There are so many distractions that pull our eyes away from the goal of life, Jesus Christ. This book follows the journey of a man who has fought and is fighting those distractions. We see inside a heart that pursues intimacy with God and the tracks to follow him into action for our own pursuit.
—**Charlie Hall**, worship leader

Through his personal journey, Dwayne teaches us that the one thing to be prized above all else is knowing God and living in the knowledge of His love for us. This is a powerful, challenging, and honest book that will inspire you to walk more closely with Jesus.
—**Mike Pilavachi**, leader and founder of the Soul Survivor youth movement

BOLDLY PURSUING ALL THAT MATTERS
DWAYNE ROBERTS

ONE
THING

[RELEVANTBOOKS]

Published by Relevant Books
A division of Relevant Media Group, Inc.

www.relevantbooks.com
www.relevantmediagroup.com

© 2005 Relevant Media Group

Design by Relevant Solutions
Cover design by Mark Arnold
Interior design by Jeremy Kennedy, Ryan Skjervem

Relevant Books is a registered trademark of Relevant Media Group, Inc., and is
registered in the U.S. Patent and Trademark Office.

Library of Congress Control Number: 2005934269
International Standard Book Number: 0-9763642-5-5

For information or bulk orders:
RELEVANT MEDIA GROUP, INC.
100 SOUTH LAKE DESTINY DR. STE. 200
ORLANDO, FL 32810
407-660-1411

06 07 08 09 9 8 7 6 5 4 3 2 1

Printed in the United States of America

To Jennifer, Sydney, Chloe, and Elijah

In writing this book I have laid out some principles that, if walked out, will cause you to be happy in your old age—you might not be incredibly rich, but you will be happy. I make a commitment that I will endeavor to walk these out all the days of my life, and I pray that as a family we can walk this journey together. At the end of the day though, it will be you coming to the same conclusions that I have come to. The one thing is the only necessary thing.

CONTENTS

ACKNOWLEDGMENTS

Thank you to Josh and Abby,
for helping with the book,
and to the IHOP family.

FOREWORD

When Dwayne came to Kansas City in 1998 with his wife, Jennifer, he didn't like to pray. Dwayne and Jennifer had been on the mission field for ten years, and as you'll read in chapter 1, Dwayne was burned out and disillusioned with ministry. He loved the Lord. He wanted to serve the Lord. He yearned to see others come to a saving relationship with Christ. However, after years of trying so hard to "do" ministry, feeling like the fruits of his labor were not what they should be, he contemplated giving up. He knew something was wrong, he knew something was missing, but he didn't know what that "something" was or how to change it.

It was at this point in their lives that I became acquainted with Dwayne and Jennifer. Despite the fact that he didn't like to pray, Dwayne was led by the Holy Spirit in 1999 to go on staff at the International House of Prayer (IHOP) as an intercessory missionary. He was initially reluctant because he had never found prayer to be all that effective. Dwayne wanted to get back out there and "work" for God instead of sitting around praying. Yet, in the way that only God can lead us, he was led to stay and pray.

Dwayne was instrumental in establishing IHOP-KC from its inception, and his journey with God from 1999 until now has been one wonderful discovery. I've seen Dwayne come from a burned-out missionary, ready to quit ministry, to an on-fire lover of God. Today I see a man growing into his calling, established in God, gaining understanding of who he is before God, and what his ultimate purpose is. This man has grown into one of the key senior leaders throughout this missions base, carrying a great amount of our responsibilities, values, and vision.

Dwayne and Jennifer live out a unique and influential partnership. Together, they are equal partners in ministry and live out their callings of leadership side by side. As their good friend and fellow intercessor, I have had the privilege of watching their journey and have witnessed a transformation within their lives and hearts. Even while preaching from platform to platform, Dwayne humbly credits Jennifer as the better speaker. She is an anointed communicator and powerful intercessor, with a vibrant spirit and passionate heart.

Dwayne and Jennifer have three dynamic children: Sydney, Chloe, and Elijah, who will undoubtedly surpass the steps of passionate pursuit that have been walked out before them. This couple continues to amaze me as they raise their children within the environment of the House of Prayer, creating wholehearted lovers of God. Dwayne and Jennifer are living strategic lives after Jesus as they feast upon the Word of God, instruct others into truth, and pursue lifestyles of wholehearted abandonment.

The insight, wisdom, passion, and truth contained within this book are the result of Dwayne's revelation that no ministry, career, reputation, or amount of earthly success was ever meant to be our primary purpose or goal in life. Knowing our God, being known by Him, and being in close relationship with Him is our primary purpose in life. This is why He created us. This is what we are here for. We were not created by God to "do." We were created to "be." We were created to be with God.

Psalm 27:4 says, "One thing I have desired of the Lord, that will I seek: that I may dwell in the house of the Lord all the days of my life, to behold the beauty of the Lord, and to inquire in His temple" (NKJV). In this psalm, David is communicating that he discovered his primary purpose in life was to "be" with God—nothing more and nothing less. David understood that all of life is about one thing. That's it. He somehow reduced everything in his life to its lowest common denominator, to discover that it was all about one thing: *desire for the Lord*. Dwayne Roberts has done the same.

This idea of being with God as our primary reason for existence is not a new idea. However, as a whole, the Church has somehow lost this reality along the way. Never have people in the Western world been so hungry for truth, so desperate for something more, so willing to do anything to fill the emptiness inside them; and never have they remained so unfulfilled. I believe we were created to hunger and to long for more. The problem is not in the longing or hungering; the problem is that only God can satisfy our deepest need.

Beloved, God delights in you! Just as you are. He loves you, has always loved you, and will continue loving you forever. When we realize this and let the truth of it penetrate our hearts, the automatic response is one of love for Him. Emotion is not something we have to conjure up or force to happen. The natural response to being loved, desired, and wanted is to love in return. Understanding this will change your life. Dwayne writes that having a vibrant heart energized by the smile of God and sustained by the understanding that He delights in you is the "better" we've all been looking for. Not only is it better, it is the one thing—the only thing—necessary to all of life.

This book truly is about what it means to be a person of "one thing" and how we cultivate a life of "one thing." It is about the transformation that takes place within your innermost being when you grasp the truth that God delights in you, likes you, and wants to be with you. It is about the pure joy of prayer when you know that you're not just talking *at* God, but talking *with* Him, and He's talking with you. This is a book about the wonder of simply "being" with God. It is a book that reminds us that our greatest reward in life—the only reward worth seeking—is God Himself.

As I said in the beginning, *One Thing* is for everyone. For all those who have thought that there must be more to a life in God than they're experiencing ... for all those who've wondered where it all went wrong in their relationship with God ... for all those who've tried and tried and tried and then tried some more to go further in God, only to feel they've gone backward ... for all those who hunger and long for more intimacy with God, but never seem to feel fulfilled ... for all those who are ready to give up because it all seems too difficult ... for all those who want to enjoy prayer, rather than endure it, but can't seem to break through ... this book is for all of you. Not only does Dwayne demonstrate God's plan for us to be people of "one thing," he shows us how to pursue it, putting desire into action.

One Thing is very personal. Dwayne shares candidly from his own life—both the struggles and the victories. It is a very "real" book. In addition to sharing his personal journey in God, he uses examples of men and women from the Bible who also discovered the delight of being a person of "one thing"—David, the Apostle Paul, Mary of Bethany, the prophet Isaiah, and even Jesus Himself—to illustrate that it is possible for each of us to be people of "one thing," and how, at the end of the day, that is all God wants us to be. The Bible is God's love story to each of us. Dwayne does a remarkable job of weaving Scripture, personal experience, and revelation gained through hours and hours before the Lord to communicate this truth in a powerful, passionate, and realistic way.

As Dwayne's friend and as a person who is committed to a life of pursuing one thing, I am delighted to see this book published. I encourage you to read this book over and over again, asking the Holy Spirit to allow the truth and the passion within it to go deep into your innermost being. As you read this book, ask God to pierce your heart with the knowledge of His love for you and His delight in you. Ask Jesus to help you simply "be" with Him. Then, give this book to your friends and family. Give it to somebody at work or church. Give it to your neighbors. Give it to unbelievers and new believers. Give it to anyone you can think of. They will come away from this book with much hope, much understanding, much relief, and much desire to pursue God, His Son, and a life of "one thing."

Mike Bickle
Director, International House of Prayer–Kansas City

INTRODUCTION →

Most everything in the Western world is aimed at arresting your attention. Every advertisement, every piece of entertainment, and every gotta-have-it item has taken aim at the core of who you are—one giant hunger. And they are offering their answer: fascination. In one form or another, each one says, "We know who you are, and we have what you want." Ironically, they are more honest about our hearts than the Church has been.

On one hand, we have hunger. We are driven, we desire, and we want. Beyond the basic needs of sustenance and shelter, this hunger is the undeniably real part of us that makes us human. For some reason, we don't just settle—we want the finer things in life. In the same way that any old antelope would feed a cheetah, soybean burgers and water will fill our stomachs. But steak and lobster would be better. I've never run across a disgruntled ant that has had enough with foraging and carrying stuff. Any job will pay the bills, but wouldn't that other position be much better? And while a bear gets one new coat a year, we'd like to have a few new outfits each season. It has little to do with snobbery, greed, or gluttony, but with the eternal hunger God has put within us. Every once in a while we certainly get a bit off track with how we allow this hunger to materialize in our lives, but that doesn't mean it is either evil or non-existent. It is just misguided and in need of an adjustment.

On the other hand, we have fascination. We are filled with a deep hunger, and the bulk of our time, energy, and resources is spent trying to satisfy that hunger with a lasting fascination. If desire is what drives us, fascination is what keeps us. All sorts of futile pleasures besides God are stealing the heart of this generation, which brings me to why I wrote this book.

After talking with so many inside and outside of the Church, I can identify a pattern starting to emerge. It seems that both the saved and unsaved are crying out for truth, for reality, for the ability to know and feel what is truly eternal. They want something of eternity to fascinate them. Whether or not they will say it this way, they want God.

Through the centuries, the saints of old have been satisfied by God. But more than that, they have been completely won over to the point of leaving everything else in order to have Him as their reward, as their one thing. At this time in history, I want to invite you into the same journey. Wherever you are in life, don't cheat yourself—your calling is to be fascinated by God Himself.

Not just facts and trivia about Him, not a ten-step program, not the coolest way to do worship or church ... God Himself. Anything less is misguided foraging and second-rate soybean burgers.

Spiritual hunger is at an all-time high. Unlike any other period in history, this young adult generation is universally hungry for spiritual enlightenment. It's evident from the sheer numbers. Right now, Islam is the fastest-growing religion in America. The kicker is that many of the converts at one point pursued Jesus. This is not some silly competition to get bigger numbers; it is an alarming reality: in the process of pursuing God, while they were in the Church, these people lost their way. This is a horrifying thought. My fear is that they had a glimpse of God and understood salvation, but the Church fed them shallow programs intended to keep them in the pews instead of empowering them and helping them learn how to touch God Himself.

Spiritual hunger isn't the only thing measuring off the charts. Right now, discontentment and disillusionment within the Church are astronomical. According to the Barna Research Group (*www.barna.org*), the percentage of people who are believers but are not attending church is the highest it has ever been, especially in the twenty-five and younger crowd. Young adults are losing hope in the Church and in what they are hearing from that mute and powerless structure, even though the options as far as what church to join are endless: the one with the plasma screen or the one that meets in the local bar, the megachurch or the "our four and no more," the home group or the subculture ministry. I am not calling you to do church any particular way. I am inviting you to experience Jesus in the midst of church today. I think that church is vital to spiritual health, but in the midst of all our doing and going, throughout all the busyness of life, there is still only one thing necessary: experiencing the joys of touching Jesus.

I am the father of three amazing children—Sydney, Chloe, and Elijah—and they have won my heart. To me, there would be no greater pain than to one day see them not loving Jesus. I can make them wash behind their ears and pick up their toys, but I cannot do anything to control or manipulate their hearts to love Him. I can do my best to live godly, humbly, and vulnerably before them. I can tell them about Jesus. And I can pray that the Holy Spirit would reveal Himself, for I am sure that if they see Him clearly, they will fall in love with Him. In this book I am sharing the same things with you that I share with them. It has been proven through the ages: when energy is put into pursuing God, the heart touches Him and is satisfied. If my kids get this, I will be happy.

As I write this, I am in the International House of Prayer in Kansas City, and my eight-year-old, Sydney, is at the 6:00 a.m. prayer meeting with me. When I went in to wake her this morning, she jumped up and asked, "It's time?" The night before, without any prompting, she had asked me to wake her up so she could come to the prayer meeting. I am confident that if she continues to pursue Jesus with this kind of hunger, she will be fascinated with God for eternity.

There is one thing necessary. There is one thing fascinating. Your hunger is real; now let your fascination be eternal.

I QUIT!

01

TODAY WAS DIFFERENT

I was in the midst of leading about 150 people in a missions outreach in downtown Budapest, Hungary. It was an incredibly intense period of time in my life. We were two days into it when I began falling apart.

I had a passion for evangelism, and I had been a leader with Youth With A Mission (YWAM) for quite some time, but this morning was different. The day before, my wife, Jennifer, and I were involved in a car accident. The day before that, somebody had broken into our car—so far, not highlights of our week.

And this morning I woke up so sick that I couldn't get out of bed. All in all, it had been a pretty rough week, although the rough times had been going on for more than that week—so long, in fact, that I couldn't really recall a time when I felt good, at peace, satisfied. And I knew this was not good for a leader in ministry.

We had a great apartment in downtown Budapest, so I couldn't complain; fourteen-foot vaulted ceilings, three big doors that opened up so you could walk into a huge kitchen, and a large office area. There was even a loft. It was one of my favorite places to live because I felt submerged in the culture, and that's a good thing for a missionary to feel. Maybe I could actually be "a light in the darkness," maybe I could even have an impact, and then maybe "Dwayne Roberts' International Ministry" could finally take off, and I would be invited to speak to millions in the stadiums of the world! (Needless to say, any dreams began to stem more from my ego than my heart for ministry.) But no, not this morning; this morning was different—in a bad way.

As I lay in my bed, sick as could be, upset that someone had broken into our car, feeling the weight of leading a major YWAM outreach, and slightly depressed, I began to talk honestly with God. Now when I say *with*, what I mean is that I talked *at* Him because I can't say that I expected Him to answer any more than I expected a friend's answering machine to have a real conversation with me. For all I knew, I was just leaving a message, and I didn't have the slightest expectation of a call back. I was really just trying to process the "life equation."

I had expected to be at a certain point in my life by then, and it just hit me ... I was never going to get there. As I tried to match up all the encouragement and kudos I had received along my spiritual journey with the reality of where I was, I realized how far I was from the expectations of everyone, including myself. So I continued processing my life equation. But the more I did, the more frustrated I became with my own lack of accomplishment, turning it into a tangible amount of hopelessness.

You know the feeling ... It's when the "could haves" don't matter because it's already too late, too far away, too much for you to do on your own. It's the very end of a long road that you began on years ago, only now—after years of thankless, rewardless travel—you realize that you were going in the wrong direction. It's the day of the big project that counts as half of the semester's grade, and your computer has inherited a self-annihilating virus. It's the morning of the big promotion interview with the district manager, and you were up all night preparing and stressing, forgot to set your alarm, and already are an hour and forty-five minutes late. It's the day you were going to take care of the (expired) tags on your car, but the cop has already put the ticket on your windshield. It's the space flight that has already taken off, but as it heads toward a blazing star, someone discovers that the trajectory is all wrong ... hopelessness.

I was pouring my life out in ministry, even living cross-culturally on the mission field, but my inner man, my spirit, was not being satisfied. I was feeling the weight of my own personal longing but knew that it would never be fulfilled. I was calling people to God, but not even sure I was enjoying Him. When I closed my eyes, I didn't feel Him near, didn't feel rejuvenated, didn't feel life coming to me. I felt hopeless. As a supposed ambassador of God, I knew there was something not right with this equation.

Somewhere along the way, there's that moment when you realize you just made a huge, life-altering decision. As soon as you hit that point, it stuns you, and you just stand there, afraid for a split second because you don't know where to go or what to do. One single thought overwhelms you: I have already taken the first step, maybe even the first several steps. If I turn back now, I will at least know what tomorrow will look like. But that's the problem, isn't it? You really do know that tomorrow will be the same. And the day after that. And the month after that. And the years that follow will be a big mishmash of blurred, boring, disconnected pictures—no life, no vibrancy, no real heart-connect with anything that has happened.

I had already made up my mind. Why should I continue on in "ministry" like this? I'd rather be back in North America with my house, picket fence, and family car, working as a garbage man. I'm done with the ministry—I quit!

DESTINED FOR MINISTRY

Quitting the ministry was never something I intended to check off my to-do list. As long as I can remember, I have felt a profound calling on my life. You see, I wasn't supposed to live. My mother had several miscarriages before getting pregnant with me, so there was a lot of concern about whether I would actually live. Then a few months into the pregnancy, her parents were killed in a terrible car accident. The doctor seriously doubted that I would make it full-term because of all that was going on in my mother's world. Later, some major complications arose during labor. When I came out, I wasn't breathing well, so I was rushed to the neonatal intensive care unit and put on an incubator. My rough entry into this world reinforced my mother's belief that God had something special for my life.

From a young age, my parents began speaking to me about my destiny and future. They continuously assured me that there

4

was a calling over my life for ministry, so naturally I grew up believing I would preach the Gospel behind a pulpit. I went through high school, with all its normal tests and trials, trying to fit the stereotype of a good believer. All the while I kept looking forward to walking out my future in God.

DESTINED FOR YWAM

Right before high school graduation, as my athletic destiny would have it, I ripped my ACL to shreds, thanks to my involvement in football and skiing. After a couple of surgeries, which slowed my "life progress" down quite a bit, I finally got a job delivering milk to grocery stores. And because of this turn of events, I met my wife, Jennifer, at the 1988 Winter Olympics in Alberta, Canada. I always like to say that I was a downhill skier and she was a figure skater. Of course, neither of those are true, but with our raw Olympic talent, it could have been.

Our churches teamed up to do an evangelism outreach together, and along the way Jennifer officially introduced me to the ministry called Youth With A Mission. I vaguely recalled hearing of a couple people who had participated in YWAM, but I was under the strong impression that I was on a one-way trip to an "official" missions-focused Bible school. I didn't think I had any other options. Although YWAM sounded pretty cool, I didn't give it a second thought.

One morning at church, my dad was preaching on marriage or carnality—I can't really remember which—and I was doing my best to sit there and pay attention. Wham! Out of nowhere something happened ... I hesitate attempting to explain it; I just knew that the Lord was speaking to me clearly about direction. This was the first time it had ever happened, so I was a bit shaken up because of the shock of receiving an undeniable prompting from God. The thought dropped deep inside my heart and lodged itself there. I could not deny the impact it had on me.

That happened in the springtime. I remember, because He said that in the fall I would be in Amsterdam, Holland. I was so confused, but I couldn't shake it, so I filled out an application for YWAM. They called back and said the school was full, but they would put me on a waiting list. Fast-forward a few months to the second week of August. I got a phone call, and it was YWAM. "A space has opened up. Do you still want to come?"

I found myself in Holland for a three-month session at a Discipleship Training School (DTS) that focused on God, His character, evangelism, various cultures, building relationships, and how to connect all those dots together—preparing me for a three-month outreach (missions trip) which would immediately follow. I got my first taste of European life there: walking the streets, shopping outdoors, hitting the cafes, strolling along the canals late at night—I loved Europe! It felt so right, like I was supposed to settle over there. I loved experiencing cross-cultural life. I was excited, thinking this was the place from which "Dwayne Roberts' International Ministry" would launch. I envisioned the big lights, brochures, the whole bit. Jennifer started DTS three months after I did, and our programs crossed paths, so we spent a week together in Amsterdam.

My six months with YWAM helped solidify my future in regard to ministry, as I found myself celebrating every morning I got to wake up and pursue missions. I returned home to Calgary, Canada, but felt like I was supposed to continue my involvement with YWAM, so a few months later I returned to Amsterdam. Jennifer came back to Amsterdam as well, and soon we started dating and eventually got married.

Jennifer and I decided to devote our energy to the missions work the Lord had put on our hearts, and by the time we were finished with YWAM ten years later, we had done some wild and crazy things. We had gone to more than thirty-five nations. I was only twenty years old when I led my first team into Liberia, West Africa, in the middle of civil war. I thought I was completely radical, on the edge, living life to the full. I lost fifteen pounds in a month. We were going hard ... preaching the Gospel, leading outreach teams.

We spent our first five years in Amsterdam. But as time went on, in our hearts we felt that a change was coming, and we received word about YWAM pioneering work in Budapest. Instead of looking deeper, we were naïve enough to believe that the "model" we were following in Amsterdam was what was wrong. It can't be us, we're doing all the right stuff ... it must be the way we're doing it, so let's try something different. How about a new start-up? Instead of leading outreach teams to multiple countries, we decided to live in one location and concentrate on one people group. We were convinced that the missions model in Budapest would be the real deal; we would actually get in on the ground floor of a pioneering work and be instrumental in building it up. Little did we know that we would be trying a new version of the same old song, which would lead us back to the same frustration. Second verse, same as the first.

While we may have missed the point the Lord was trying to hit home, we were sincere in our efforts and honorable in our actions, and God, in His mercy, started to cause some desires to rise from the depths of my heart. It was there in Budapest that I really began to preach the Gospel with power and authority. I was desperate to see Him touch people, and I instinctively knew it would not happen without some measure of visible power. We targeted a neighborhood where we were going to share the Gospel, and I threw my life into it with every ounce of energy I had.

FROM ROCK STAR TO DISILLUSIONED

Jennifer and I were running hard in missions and truly longing to see people come to the Lord. It was at this time that a friend of mine wanted to put together a band and use it as an evangelism tool. He was a great songwriter with honest lyrics. We figured that the combination of his musicianship and my organizational skills might be able to open some doors. So he headed up the band and taught me to play bass. I worked on getting access to places that weren't necessarily receptive to the Gospel but would love an American band to headline.

We became bona fide rock stars (at least in some people's minds—and definitely in ours). We toured all over. The crazy things was, at that point in time, if you spoke English, had a band, and traveled all over Eastern Europe, they assumed you were a big dog. We were doing radio spots and TV appearances during the day and playing in a bunch of clubs at night. We would play in three or four clubs to get our name out there, and then we'd rent our own facility where we would do a concert and then preach ... Romania, Sarajevo, Yugoslavia, all over Serbia, down into Greece, any place we could.

During this season, I envisioned the Gospel having power on it. I wanted to have great impact, to see lives radically changed. We saw despair in places like Sarajevo, Croatia, and Serbia. We drove through villages and found homes completely leveled; bombs had gone off, creating crater after crater. It was a war zone. One little six-year-old girl showed us her belly, revealing a spider's web-looking scar where a sniper had shot her. There was complete despair everywhere. We heard stories about the violation of young women that would make your stomach convulse, and we earnestly desired the Gospel to have impact in that place. We wanted it to break through the injustices and the deep emotional anguish within every soul, and to raise the low places of despair to a height that could only be attributed to God. We wanted Jesus to be seen for all He truly is. We were set on instilling joy and hope in every misery-engulfed person. It sounded simple enough—there were plenty of opportunities.

I was at these concerts, preaching the Gospel, wanting to do it with energy, with the anointing of the Holy Spirit. But the amount of frustration I felt day after day continuously ate away at my boldness and drive. I would preach, but it would just barely get off my tongue before it splatted on the ground like an eighty-pound wet fish. Every word felt undermined by the reality of my own life, by the barrenness of my own heart, by the utter lack in my own spiritual walk. We'd have anywhere from fifty to one thousand people gathered, but the message would barely fumble out of my mouth. It would fall short, and I would feel the inadequacy of it all—my inadequacy in it all.

There was something very personal about what was going on. We'd see perhaps three or four people come to know the Lord, but when we came back six months later, we couldn't find them. The impact was simply not lasting. I'm not saying there was no fruit during that season, but it certainly was not what I had dreamed of. I was giving all my energy to something, only to have it feel like another exercise in futility. Now, it was definitely not this bad on a daily basis, hour by hour, but at different occasions I was overwhelmed by a recurring feeling: why do I continue on when it simply is not working? It was a true, valid burden that I needed to deal with head-on.

After our first daughter, Sydney, was born in Budapest, life became more of a challenge. Priorities and responsibilities shifted. The things I wanted to do began to come second to the things I needed to do. No longer did I want to take my little girl on a trip and sleep on a back porch one night, in some hotel in who-knows-where the next, and then back to another porch. Being a father was a whole new dynamic.

Now fast-forward a few weeks. And a few more. Log a couple memories in the brain and add a few more weeks to the mix. Toss in a month here and there, and I began to lose track of lots of things, but my heart discerned the important parts ... something was taking place in my inner man—namely, a certain amount of disillusionment.

As young Christians, so many of us throw ourselves into one form or another of service, all the while believing that our inner man (our spirit and our heart) will be taken care of and satisfied because of our actions. In some ways it's like striking a deal with God: I'll do this as long as You do that. It almost sounds reasonable or fair. We clock in and start keeping track, hoping that He'll make the math work out to our benefit in the end. *Tit for tat, scratch my back and I'll scratch Yours, keep the blessings coming and I'll keep on serving.*

We say that God is really our one true desire and that intimacy is always first in our life, but let's be honest. Isn't ministering (especially in public or where recognition just may come our way) a lot more fun than whatever intimacy really is? On the whole, does it seem the Church is more interested in ministering publicly or in communing privately with the Lord and then doing acts of secret power and unknown kindness?

And what is this intimacy thing anyway? It has been the Christian buzzword since the early '90s, but I dare say that it has yet to permeate the average believer's life. Let's take one facet of intimacy—study and meditation—and ask a question: Do we generally study out of unrestrained desire to encounter Jesus and know Him in a greater way, or do we leave our time of gleaning mostly excited that we have acquired more knowledge? Do we approach our devotional times with a stopwatch and a groan, or with a heart brimming with the passion simply to be with God? Is it just like your day job, or is it the long-awaited moment of lavishing and lingering between a bridegroom and His bride? Do you even like it? What if you still had to do it but never gained another ounce of knowledge ... would you enjoy it then? Would it satisfy?

Many of us, including myself, have thought that doing some kind of Christian work or ministering in a particular way somehow equals having a life in God. We have believed that actions and doing, doing, doing would somehow satisfy the deep longing for the divine that our Heavenly Father placed inside us. But becoming a pastor is not the end-all, and neither is becoming a missionary, apostle, prophet, church planter, soccer coach, retail employee, or engineer. The primary purpose of our spiritual life is not ministry, but rather knowing God and being in a relationship with Him. Now, I'm not saying that the Great Commission is anything less than it really is; remember, I am an evangelist at heart, and my desire is for multitudes to come into the kingdom. But that day in Budapest, I quit because my spirit was famished, and no amount of ministry fed me.

As I said, I had a ministry. But for all the hard work I put in, the hours I spent, and the Scriptures I quoted, I couldn't understand the phenomenal lack of fruit. The equation wasn't working. The negative was somehow more than the positive. I was doing my part, so what happened to His? There was only minimal ministerial success. It was the sucker punch to the gut of my Christian dreams, which led me into a very real despair. I already believed that there was something wrong with the ministry equation. Now question marks were beginning to appear over not just a part of the ministry, but the entirety of my approach to ministry.

But now, as I sit here and consider all the components to this divine story, I realize something: if I had truly been fruitful in ministry, it would have squelched a certain amount of disillusionment and hunger I was feeling. Dangerously, I would have believed that a successful ministry equaled a vibrant life in God.

I admit that there was also a certain amount of boredom with God. Nowadays the typical pastor prays about five to seven minutes a day, and I'd have to raise my hand and say that my lifestyle couldn't claim any more than that. In public I would call myself an evangelist, a preacher, a proclaimer of the Gospel— all the while praying only five to seven minutes a day—and then bang my head against the wall, wondering why there was no impact in ministry. Four hundred and twenty seconds of prayer at the most, and then wondering what the problem was; questioning God as if He had failed to pull through. To my brain, it just wasn't making sense. I wondered, *How much do I have to do for You to respond?*

So in my bed in Budapest that morning, I decided, *Something is massively missing; something is really, really, really wrong. I quit. I refuse to go on like this.* That was a defining moment. That morning was different.

Not much changed in my immediate circumstances, but I had been honest with the Lord. *This is not working, and I want some help.* At the end of the day, I really don't think that my journey is that much different from anyone else's. God had me on this journey to bring me to some conclusions. Whether you are in college, starting your career, working as a teacher/pastor/musician, whether you are a regular Joe or a super-spiritual Christian, you will find that the questions are all the same. When it comes to spiritual issues, you may also find yourself arriving at similar conclusions. It is exactly what I needed to go through to become the man He wanted me to be. It was not too much or too little. It was precisely what I needed because at this point I actually started walking out life in God.

CHANGING THE MODEL

Jennifer and I began a dialogue with the Lord at about the three-year mark of our almost-five years in Budapest. We again came to think that the "model," the way we were doing things, was what was wrong. Maybe a parachurch organization is not something we should be involved with ... perhaps we should be involved with planting churches instead. Ah yes, that sounds about right. After we came to that conclusion, a series of events followed, which you might call "divine interventions." We weren't necessarily correct in our naïve assumption about the model being wrong, but this was the path the Lord used to reach us. He wanted us to exhaust some options while awakening a fierce hunger for Him alone.

The entire band returned to the United States with the understanding that we would be based out of Atlanta and still travel a lot. During this time Jennifer and I made a decision to step out of missions for a season to let things settle. This was a massive change for us because we never pictured ourselves living in the United States; we assumed we would be doing ministry in third-world countries for the rest of our lives. I hooked up with a friend in Athens, Georgia, and we decided to try our hands at being missions pastors. The general idea was to build a network of small groups (like cell groups or small home churches) with the intention of going back to the mission field with these same people to plant churches.

Meanwhile, because we had made some commitments in Europe, the whole band had to fly back and do a music festival in southern Hungary. When we arrived, we either sold or gave everything away—our car, furniture, apartment, clothes, you name it. As soon as we were done at the festival, we were moving to Georgia. Jump or die, cut the rope, burn the ship, all or nothing. There was no turning back now, mainly because we didn't really have anywhere to turn. Either God would pull through for us crazy kids or we were toast.

If you've ever been at an outdoor music festival, you'll recall several things. First, there are a lot of people. Second, there is usually a lot of food. Now do the math: people who eat and drink need a place to ... sleep isn't what I was thinking. So we were out digging toilets in a field for the festival when we got an email from my mission-pastor friend in Georgia. He only wrote one quick paragraph: "I know we had a whole plan mapped out, but sorry, I'm moving ... the door's closed." Boom—just like that.

A day later Jennifer got into a car accident. She was turning, and a guy on the Hungarian highway slammed into her. The policeman took her passport and cited her despite her innocence. Her back was all out of whack, and she was in a lot of pain, but we both felt an amazing sense of peace. Of course, we had no idea where we were going to live in four days or what we were going to do, but we were leaving the band to give the church-planting model a whirl. Different model, big plans, we felt like we were stepping up the spiritual ladder. If you remember the theme song to *The Jeffersons*, sing along with me ... "Well we're movin' on up to the east side, to a dee-luxe apartment in the sky, we're movin' on up to the east side. We've finally got a piece of the pie."

In the midst of the craziness, a small group from Kansas City, Missouri, showed up in Hungary as the speakers of the festival. I felt drawn toward one guy in particular, so I introduced myself. We exchanged the usual pleasantries, but I really started to take notice when he told me about a recent sleepless night. He said, "Oh, the Lord woke me up about two weeks ago and told me I would be meeting a man named Dwayne. I just never thought it would be in a foreign country." To hear that the Lord would wake up a total stranger in the middle of the night, tell him my name, and send him to another country to meet me brought a massive amount of peace to my heart. He cares—God really does care about us!

The gentleman didn't share much with me and Jennifer, but somehow he got our attention in a major way. He said, "You're in transition." It wasn't the most amazing piece of insight, but it brought a tremendous peace to us, knowing that God knew our name. And that's all we needed to know. It was just like when something really horrible happens to you and you find yourself surrounded by well-meaning, good-hearted people who sometimes say the wrong things: "It'll get better ... Just don't blame yourself ... You are so courageous for coming out in public so soon after ... You must be really mad at God for this ... I guess God just wanted it this way ... Whatever you do, just don't give up on your faith ..." While they mean well (and they undoubtedly do), it pricks that painful spot in your heart one more time.

Then a breath of fresh air comes through—a good friend looks you in the eye and, with the most profound sincerity, says simply, "I love you." You realize that was all you wanted to hear. Nothing could have comforted you more, and nothing more was needed; no theological affirmations, no grand theories, and certainly no clichés could have touched you with such tender impact.

In that season of our lives, the tangible comfort of God came to us in the form of a simple understanding: He knows us, and our future is secure. This morning was different.

A SEASON IN KANSAS CITY

It was through the relationship we developed with the group from Kansas City that we decided to move there. We intended to do a year of study at the Bible school and then return to the mission field. That was our plan and focus.

We arrived in town in August of 1998. For the first few weeks the buzz among the students centered around a certain class. "Have you taken the class yet? It's amazing ... It'll change you ... I fell in love with God again ... It's on the Song of Solomon, and Mike Bickle is teaching it." I was a little confused, but all the talk really grabbed my attention. How could an archaic story with a bunch of weird flowers and fruit touch so many people this way? I signed up and began taking the class, but it went right over my head. We would go phrase by phrase through each verse, cross-reference it with other Bible verses, and throw in some thoughts from a few of the old saints with strange names. Like a Microsoft program at an Apple convention or a vegan at a barbecue, I was lost. I did not understand the excitement of those around me.

I would go home after class and tell Jennifer, "I just don't understand what this guy is talking about. That whole chapter sounded like we were reading a shampoo bottle!" I stuck it out for the entire semester, but I still didn't get it no matter what I tried. It just didn't connect with me, or I didn't connect with it—it had to be one of the two.

During that semester, Mike began to talk about starting a "House of Prayer." We didn't know what he was talking about, but all of a sudden the whole school was buzzing about this International House of Prayer that would be right in Kansas City (IHOP-KC). I didn't have any idea what it would look like. All I knew was that as Mike stepped down to run IHOP full-time, our old boss from YWAM was coming to be the senior pastor. This gentleman had been the top dog in Amsterdam, and now he was coming to Kansas City. In my mind, it couldn't get much better.

To make a long story short, the International House of Prayer opened, and it began to catch a couple of my heart strings. In particular, two ideas struck me as simple and profound all at once: praying for the Gospel to be powerful and effective, and the idea of unmistakable anointing when the Gospel is preached. First you pray, then you preach, and God does stuff. The Holy Spirit pierces hearts and opens up the revelation of the knowledge of God, and revival is loosed; hands are laid on the sick, and they actually get healed. My heart was being stirred, and I was being awakened to that reality again. What I experienced at the House of Prayer reminded me of back-in-the-day stories my dad used to tell me about revivals and the power of the Gospel.

My heart was being moved. I once again possessed the desire to preach with true authority and see miracles just as I had longed for back in Hungary. I had read Acts time and time again and wondered why there was such a discrepancy between the events there and those in my own life. I wanted what they had: the relationship with God, the anointing in preaching, the life-changing miracles. Gently, the Lord began to prod me in the direction of the House of Prayer, giving me a passion for twenty-four/seven worship and intercession.

At first I resisted. *You want me to be a missionary who just prays? But I don't even like to pray!* And I didn't. There was no denying it. A daily five-minute prayer life had not convinced me that it was truly beneficial. It may have been necessary at times, but it mostly seemed like a duty I was supposed to perform, akin to doing the dishes—you only cleaned them if all the other dishes were dirty and you really needed a clean fork and plate. In the same way, you only prayed when all hope was lost and you really needed God to come through. Sure, I knew I was supposed to pray, but I had never really invested my heart in it. I wouldn't go so far as to claim that it was a waste of time, but it certainly felt more like a burden and an obligation than a heartfelt craving. I couldn't even have quoted you five verses that exhort us to pray. *Of all the things You could have asked me to do, Lord, why did You pick prayer? Are You sure this is a wise move?*

It was in the midst of asking this question that Mike approached us. "Why don't you come join staff at the House of Prayer?" "No thanks. I think we're probably going to end up working with our friend from YWAM because he does missions, small groups, church planting ... that's our kind of thing." We were still under the impression that the model was wrong and that the church-planting concept was the direction we should be headed. Well, as soon as we said "no" to Mike, everything began to crumble, which set us back to "praying." *Oh heavenly Father, all our plans seem to be falling apart. I guess we don't have anywhere else to turn at the moment besides You. And by the way, we really, really need You to come through this time.* Yeah, I know. Pretty weak prayer, right? That would be a good summary for most of my prayer times; they were consistently weak. It may even be a pretty accurate summary of the prayer time for most believers. But that is changing. The Lord is doing something spectacular. He has begun to do it in me, and He is committed to seeing it through to its glorious end in you as well.

Since joining IHOP in July of 1999, my prayer times have been getting a bit healthier. I am no longer plagued with hitting the five-minute brick wall because I have concluded it is not primarily about an amount of time, regardless of whether I am wondering "how long can I do this?" or "how quickly can I get this over with?" It's about connecting with God and His heart. I am finding that my times of study are more focused as well. Overall, I feel that two distinct and related things—destiny (I am going somewhere) and urgency (it is imperative that I go)— are the blessings in my recent prayer life.

Why have I taken the time to walk you through a bit of my story? What is the point? I want you to know, first of all, that it is okay not to have all the answers, but it is important to be honest about where you are in your journey. Can you relate in some ways to what I went through, to the feelings and struggles I had? You are not alone. Everyone reaches a fork in the road, a deciding point. Will you be content with the little you are experiencing with God, or will you press on for more? He gives the little because of His grace, but the deeper things are given as a reward of your diligent pursuit. Everyone gets to this point, but few treat it with the level of significance it demands. Everyone has a calling from heaven. It might be as a lawyer, nurse, or construction worker.

But that is not your end; you were not created to *do*, you were created to *be*. You were created to be His. So whether you find yourself on step one or step ten, the journey is the same. It is the journey into passion with Jesus.

Secondly, I want to spark something within you, to awaken a desire for more by letting you know, without a doubt, that there is something more ... and better. Christian service (ministry) is honorable in the sight of God, but it is not the axis on which your spiritual life should turn. A bigger and more influential ministry is not impressive to God. Your email list does not impress Him and neither does the quadrupling of your youth program. Contrary to popular opinion, getting the record deal, leading the conference, or launching the Christian TV show does not get you an honorable mention in the eternal courts. You don't get more kudos in paradise because your building was bigger than what's-his-face's down the road. And heaven does not put you on speed dial once you reach a certain point in annual sales.

Let's cut to the chase: God wants your heart completely, and that is the only thing that causes His heart to sing. A bigger and better ministry is not necessarily the "better" I am referring to, though the Lord may indeed expand your sphere of influence. A vibrant heart, energized by the smile of God and sustained by the understanding that He delights in you, is the "better." In fact, it is the one thing necessary to all of life, the wellspring from which all else flows.

I quit the ministry because it wasn't working. Sure, as far as numbers go, I was obviously unsuccessful. But that wasn't the real reason I quit. It never really is. My spirit was fading, and I was bored with God because I felt disconnected with Him—and the whole package left me truly disillusioned on many levels. My spirit was famished, and no amount of ministry fed me. I learned the hard way that doing some kind of Christian work or ministering in some way does not equal having a life in God. In case you missed it the first time, I'll say it again: ministry is not the primary purpose of our spiritual life. *God* is the purpose for our spiritual life.

The third thing I want to do is address a very real piece of our human makeup. We all feel a certain amount of emptiness. Without this emotion, would we ever be driven to search for more? Emptiness is a profound longing meant to lead us into the fullness of God. I have found that as I run to Him, He energizes my heart and satisfies my longing. I hope that sharing this journey with you has in some way validated the emptiness you sometimes feel without unnecessarily glorifying it.

I had gone round and round, trying to figure out which model to use in ministry. Only later would I discover that programs don't hold the answers for a dead heart. God was starting me over at square one: my heart needed to be alive again, and only He could make that happen. At this point of feeling quite bewildered and somewhat empty, the Lord allowed me to see a part of Him I would never have guessed existed: His delight in me.

And this day was different.

A COMMAND I CAN FOLLOW

02

YOUR REWARD IS GOD HIMSELF

"After these things the word of the Lord came to Abram in a vision, saying, 'Do not be afraid, Abram. I am your shield, your exceedingly great reward.'" —Genesis 15:1, NKJV

At one of the first prayer meetings I went to at the IHOP-KC, I heard a man pray from this verse in Genesis. This was one of the catalyst verses that started me on the journey of knowing the God of delight. Although I had been saved for most of my life, I was just now finding out that life is about loving Jesus first and foremost. Sounds simple, doesn't it? But without knowing that God delights in me, why would I want to pursue Him? The truth is, I wouldn't.

Abraham is the father of the faith that extends to the New Covenant, so the Bible spends quite a bit of time discussing his life. God raised Abraham up as a model of the principles that He wanted to bring forth in the New Covenant in a more full way, a picture of our spiritual pilgrimage at the close of human history. That's why He promised Abraham global impact touching the ends of the earth, great wealth, and a tremendous amount of favor before kings and men. He gave Abraham many dimensions of promise and reward in this age and the one to come, and it all serves as a foreshadowing of the final generation as well. But of all the rewards mentioned by the Lord, the most notable and intriguing is His promise of the exceedingly great reward of Himself.

The idea of getting a reward is very important because the way you understand your reward is significantly related to how you are motivated and your level of contentment. All of us have an idea of what our reward is; we may not articulate it clearly, but there is something we are after, and our contentment is tied to it. If someone asks what makes you fully content, you may have to stop and say, "You know, I don't know exactly how to put it." But in the language of our hearts, whether we have articulated it or not, there are things we look toward and long for that are linked to our motivation and our sense of contentment. The issue of God rewarding His people, first in time and then eternity, is a vast and important subject because it guides our emotional life right now.

The Lord appeared to Abraham in a vision and said, *Don't worry about a thing, Abraham. I am your shield, I am your source of provision, and I will personally protect you. I have promised you many things in this age and in the age to come ... tremendous impact in the nations, favor before men, tremendous riches and honor, land, influence, and a legacy for generations. But let Me make one thing clear to you, Abraham: I, Myself, am in a completely different category than all the other rewards I have promised you—I am your exceedingly great reward. There are many rewards, some of them are even great, but there is only one thing that is the exceedingly great reward.*

Jesus declared Himself to be the overwhelming, ultimate reward of the people of God both in time and in eternity. Without restraint and without hesitation, He gave Himself to His people.

As I sat listening to the intercessor's prayer that day, I felt several things taking place inside me. Initially I felt a connection among my spirit, my mind, and my heart ... somehow it all clicked. Though I didn't know how to express it with words, a tangible connection happened. My mind believed that what the intercessor was saying was true; my spirit understood that God Himself is in a category entirely greater than any other created object; and my heart longed to feel exactly what he was talking about. It was like assembling an item you just brought home from the store. The instructions say to line up part A with part B and push until you hear the click. So you push and listen until, after a few seconds of silence, the connection is the only thing you hear. As you take a step back and look at your snazzy new household item, you can't help but think, *This is how it is supposed to be.* That heart connection resonated within me, and I just knew this was how it was supposed to be. *God Himself is my reward.*

We've been bombarded from every angle by the media, and their message is always the same: you don't look good enough, smell good enough, sing well enough, dance well enough; you aren't smart enough, aren't rich enough; and even if you were, you would still be lacking because no one is perfect, least of all you. Think about it for a minute. This is the primary message of most commercials. They have convinced us that it matters if we buy this, shave that, wear this, smoke that, drink this, play that, eat this, and listen to that. Don't you ever get tired of being told you are not worth anyone's time, that you are not valuable—*that you are not delighted in?* Because that's what it boils down to.

We are constantly saturated with the "not delightful" message. We have all bought into it in one way or another—that's why it is so difficult to see—but that doesn't mean it's true. It simply means we need to find the real message, the defining message, the identity-giving message. Thankfully, a commercial can never bestow identity. Our identity is not linked to this world, which means our reward is not in this world either. Our reward is God Himself, in this life and in the life to come. He wants us. We can have Him. Our pursuit should be to gain the reward of having Jesus. This is how it is supposed to be.

Right on the heels of this heart-connect came a deep sense of regret. *If this is how it should be, then what have I been doing all these years? Have I been wasting my time? Striving after the wrong things? Have I disappointed God in the midst of my efforts?* I just wanted to take it all back—the wasted moments, the failed attempts, the heart posture of an obedient, dedicated servant instead of an overjoyed companion to God Himself. I didn't feel condemned or rejected by God because I was somehow unacceptable; I simply felt like a lot of the energy I poured out was slightly misguided. I had been doing things out of duty rather than as a natural response of an overflowing heart. My motivation, while not bad or unacceptable by any means, was just a bit off target. My aim was too low. I settled for slavish obedience instead of accepting the invitation to encounter the God of creation. I opted for bland poi and dry crackers instead of diving into the wedding buffet prepared just for me. It was as if I had won a game show and they were offering me one of three prizes: a toaster that only does one slice at a time, a puce-colored jelly bracelet, or God Himself. And somewhere along the way, I must have chosen the toaster. Because I finally realized the type of connection I could have had—the reward of having God Himself—I felt the regret of not experiencing it before then.

At the same time, hope and exhilaration swept over me. Without restraint and without hesitation, God had given Himself to me. It doesn't have to be like this. I can begin again. This can be the start of a brand new season in my life. If He said it, it has to be true! I really can have God as my reward.

DAVID'S EXAMPLE

Everyone examines his or her life in one way or another. It's only natural to take your life into account and ask all the "life equation" questions; it's an important part of being human. There comes a time in your journey to maturity when you have to be honest with yourself. *Okay, what do I want to do with my life? What am I made for? What do I want to become and how do I get there? What is important to me? What do I want to spend my energy on?*

Some people go to great measures to figure out what their pursuits will be. Lots of young adults spend the bulk of their time in college taking courses to narrow down their interests.

Others, like me, take scores of personality tests and ask friends and family for their input and wisdom.

> *"One thing I have desired of the Lord, that*
> *will I seek: That I may dwell in the house of*
> *the Lord all the days of my life, to behold*
> *the beauty of the Lord, and to inquire in His*
> *temple." —Psalm 27:4, NKJV*

In the context of Psalm 27, David was not yet king. Saul was still ruling Israel ... when he wasn't chasing David, that is. Yet in the midst of being hunted from city to city and slandered in the royal courts of his beloved homeland, David somehow found time to comment on the posturing of his heart, on the highest pursuit of his life. Interesting thing is, he narrowed it down to just one. One thing. That's it. He somehow reduced everything in his life to its lowest common denominator to discover that it was all about one thing: desire for the Lord.

He'd counted the cost and decided upon his pursuit. He took stock of his life, knowing what the future would hold for him, and set his will to see it through. Have you ever thought about how much he had to consider in order to make such an unwavering statement?

He was prophesied over and anointed as the future king of Israel when he was a teenager, so he had a lot of time to consider what it meant to be the big dog. He said, *Someday I will be the king of Israel. This means I'll have wealth. In fact, I'm going to be in control of the funds of the entire nation. I am also going to have honor. When I walk into a room, people are going to bow to me. Power: with a wave of my hand, legions will move because of my one simple decision.*

David had several years to dwell upon the responsibilities he would have and decide on his priorities. He knew he needed to have these in place before he stepped into the position of ruling. And what he chose was something greater than having the place of honor, the influence of wealth, and the position of power. He said, *There is something far greater, something more interesting, satisfying, and exhilarating than the reality of being the king of a nation.* He had made up his mind. *There is one thing I want. And it is above every other pleasure and adventure that ruling a nation has to offer.*

Because David knew that a divided aim leads to distraction, weakness, and disappointment, he set his heart with a tenacious focus. *There's one thing,* he said. *There's one thing that I want.* The amazing thing is that the individual who pursues one thing becomes successful. Distraction amidst pursuit will lead to aimlessness and wandering. But the individual who answers the call to a single pursuit will be found faithful, successful, fulfilled.

Have you ever observed a person with a gifting or propensity toward business? Personally, I find the successful ones intriguing. There's something different in their eyes: *I will be successful.* To be successful in business, you have to be single-minded. You're going to experience ups and downs, but you have to stay focused and be unwavering. Any businessman will tell you that. For me to be successful in my pursuits, I have to stay single-minded as well. It's a reality. David diligently took all things into consideration and decided on one thing to pursue.

Whether we are talking about business or spirituality, there is always a choice. David clearly saw his choice for what it was and made a resolute decision to pursue it wholeheartedly. There was no stopping him, no slowing him down. He was determined to see his journey through to the end. He was determined to have the one thing necessary; he was committed to pursuing God all the days of his life.

DESIRE AS MOTIVATION

In Matthew 13:44 the Bible tells us that Jesus called us to the exact same thing David centered his life on. "Again, the kingdom of heaven is like treasure hidden in a field, which a man found and hid; and for joy over it he goes and sells all that he has and buys that field" (NKJV). Jesus was speaking of a person who has found a great treasure. This treasure so consumes him, it becomes the joy of joys in his life, and he gives up everything—all he has—to buy one single piece of dirt in order to completely capture the treasure.

Jesus was calling for the same thing David decided to go after. He said, *I want you to posture your heart to pursue Me and My kingdom, just like this individual who sold all so he would inherit his treasure.*

But Jesus was not done with His lesson in the slightest. "Again, the kingdom of heaven is like a merchant seeking beautiful pearls, who, when he had found one pearl of great price, went and sold all that he had and bought it" (Matt. 13:45-46, NKJV). This is the story of an individual in the midst of a pursuit. He finds a pearl and is blown away by its inherent value. The pearl's beauty is far superior to anything he has encountered before; it is shockingly gorgeous. He said, *This is the one. Every day in the water, prying open oysters, has led to this—I have found what I've been seeking. I'm willing to give up everything else if I can have this one thing.*

Jesus knew they had no idea who was standing in front of them, and it pained His heart. So He put the primary commandment, the one that every Jewish person knew, into story form. Jesus said, *Can you say you know what it is like to encounter the kingdom of God, or God Himself even? Do you know what it looks like to "love the Lord God utterly"? Let Me fill in the blanks for you. The posture of this individual's heart is a great start. This man says, "The most valuable and beautiful thing is sitting right in front of me. In order to have it, I must give up everything. Even though I am a merchant (I sell these by the dozens), I am actually willing to give up everything to possess this single pearl."* Jesus is adamant about this: He wants your heart so moved by desire that you would do anything and everything to be completely His.

David learned early on that it was about one thing. When he was sixteen or seventeen years old, out on the back side of some no-name mountain looking after some sheep, he began to meditate on this beautiful God, and something inexplicable started to happen. The Holy Spirit began to bring revelation to David on the knowledge of God. The Holy Spirit began to awaken him, to open his eyes and expand his heart. David's comprehension of the Creator was being adjusted (corrected, really), and in the heart of this shepherd, desire began to take shape.

Desire began to motivate David in his pursuit. This desire actually was a longing for the knowledge of God. It had been awakened, I think, as David cultivated a specific heart posture that was able to receive revelation. We are not told exactly what revelations of God David was seeing, but as we continue, I'm going to make some speculations as to the events that may have awakened him to pursue this God. Regardless of whether or not my guesses are accurate, the truth is that revelation had touched his heart; this focus was not a result of outside influences. He didn't hear a message from a preacher on a weekly basis that drew him to the reality of pursuing God. And I don't think others were running with him arm in arm on this personal journey ... precisely because it was a personal journey. He had to do it himself, and he did it by positioning his heart to pursue a singular desire.

David possessed a yearning and a longing for this God—it was something that motivated and moved his inner man. He said, *I long for this One! This desire is so alive in me, I am willing to give up the pursuits and pleasures of this life, with the understanding that I will encounter this One. Though I'm slandered, I don't care. I want God! Something has touched my inner man, and it has awakened hunger. And not even kingship will satisfy this hunger. The only thing that will satisfy me is to touch the depths of the Creator. One thing I desire. One thing I long for—my God.* Eternity had been awakened in him, and he treasured it as an amazing gift.

We have to understand something: when revelation touches the human heart, it should not be taken lightly. Most Christians have had at least one experience when God has come and touched their heart, awakening their longing (salvation is a form of this touch). I think when those encounters happened to David, he treated them as rare experiences and devoted himself to pursuing the revelation of God that had touched His spirit. I believe this amazing gift of revelation unto the knowledge of God has been given to every one of us so that we, like David, can touch the heart of God.

Even in the middle of the desert, David was intent on touching God. When he wrote Psalm 27, he was nowhere near a city or a temple—he was being pursued by his enemies as he sneaked from cave to cave. Yet he said, *I must have more.* In his painful circumstances we might expect him to desire safety, friends, escape, refuge, or retaliation against the slander. But in the midst of being slandered and stalked, instead of wanting to find safety, defend himself, or clear his name, David rose up with the cry, *I still want God! Though everything is gone, all I want is to know my Creator! When I was looking after some sheep on the back side of that hill, I encountered the Creator. And that is what I want to go after.*

Desire was so consuming him—it was so awakened within him—that even in the midst of total calamity, desire was still the predominant influence on his decision making. It's mind-blowing. He touched God and said, "There's something fascinating about this God."

FROM DESIRE TO ACTION

In Psalm 27, the Bible tells us that David is going to act upon his desire: "that will I seek." Holy desire must lead to something. Otherwise, it will bring disillusionment: been there and tried that ... it didn't work for me.

Be honest. How many times have you heard about someone giving up on their pursuit of God? Or how many times have you seen someone chase after ministry more than after God Himself? I think it is possible that the amazing gift of the revelation of the knowledge of God was given to them. It touched them, and shame, sin, and death were broken off them. They were awakened, yet somehow they slipped into a lifestyle where they no longer pursued the knowledge of God. However, six months later, as troubles arose, they found themselves without any foundation, without any life in God. They had nothing feeding their inner man, so they gave up, saying, "I've tried God, but it never clicked for me." The result is that they leave disillusioned with the Creator who called them and gave them the amazing gift of revealing Himself to them.

But not David. He was awakened and touched on such a deep level that he actually put action and energy to the reality of going after God. He decided he was going to live outside of the norm of his society, outside of the norm of his culture, outside of the depraved value system that pervaded his society. He was going to be considered fanatical, a real radical—all because of his commitment to seek after the one thing necessary.

I know many people who sit in pews today, screaming on the inside, longing for a reality in God. But they're so stuck in their couch-potato lifestyle, watching TV, flipping through channels, surfing the Net, taking a hit, gaming, you name it ... and they're so empty on the inside. Just empty. Cold, dark, and hard hearts, longing for something more, something better. This is a picture of desire. No matter how off target, it is still a picture of desire because it is a search. Regardless of the outward display, at its core it is a search. They are looking for something that will touch them, move them, satisfy them. They are ultimately looking for God—they are simply on a misdirected search.

Now, I want you to know that I believe God responds powerfully to desire. But I believe that when you go that extra step and really pursue that desire, it enlarges the bull's eye that you're putting on your heart for the knowledge of God to pierce you. But you have to put action to your desire or you'll end up walking away, totally disillusioned and disappointed.

Even at the outset, you must know that God responds to the slightest "yes" in the human heart. Every time you say "yes" to

Him, He moves toward you. You may be covered with shame, condemned, stuck in incredible sin, but when this little "yes" is awakened in your heart, God says, "(Gasp!) I've got one!" And He begins to move toward you. You want encounter? You want the living One to walk into your room and touch you and pierce you? You want mysteries revealed to you? It will not come as you sit and just "have desire," but rather as you take three months, six months, a year, ten years to sit down and say, "I am going to give myself wholeheartedly to nothing but raw pursuit, seeking the knowledge of God."

What you're doing is enlarging the bull's eye over your heart. There is no doubt in my mind that it is the wisest thing you could ever do. As you seek God more aggressively (maybe even add in a bit of fasting), I believe it only causes you to go that much harder and faster after the Lord because you feel Him coming near you. Fasting doesn't force things to happen. No fireworks, no supernatural light show in my room, no angels or demons or anything like that. When you fast, it's not like you can bribe God to do things for you or twist His arm. However, I do know that fasting tenderizes my heart and releases revelation and insight into who God is.

Here's the economy of God, lest you think not much good comes out of it: what you experience when you fast is a little glimpse into the substance of your own heart, a little peep into the substance of His heart, and a little readjustment of your values and focus. While fasting has tangible long-term benefits, one fast won't necessarily change you from an ugly duckling to a soaring eagle. Often fasting is done because of an emergency— we need to hear from God, so we go on a three-day fast. But I suggest making it a regular part of your spiritual disciplines, and over time, it will expand your heart to be able to receive revelation, change your spiritual chemistry, and align you a bit closer with Jesus.

So, even in your pursuit, I don't want you to expect that after going hard for three weeks or six months, the Lord somehow owes you now. He pays close attention to your pursuit even when you don't feel Him near or get a massive reward instantly. It's correct to expect a reward here in this life and in the next life—as long as you don't cling more to the here than the there. The Lord is our reward; we were created for Him and His good pleasure.

Don't get lazy and give up on your lifelong pursuit of the knowledge of God if you don't feel the warm fuzzies every second of every day; this Christian journey is so much bigger than that. Take the "heroes of the faith" as an example. We read in Hebrews 11 and 12 how some of these patriarchs gave themselves all the days of their life to pursue what God had marked out for them, yet never reached that goal. But God honors them as heroes of the faith.

In your pursuit of God, you cannot—after three weeks, three months, six months, or a year—say, "Well, been there, done that, tried it." One of our favorite sayings at IHOP is that God is looking for those who will run at a marathon pace, with patient endurance and faithfulness. If you keep that hunger, and seek, press, and declare, "Creator, I know You're watching me, and I'm coming after You. I will not be denied the experience of seeing," you will find that you are positioning yourself for an encounter.

ALL THE DAYS OF MY LIFE

The next line of David's psalm is, "That I may dwell in the house of the Lord all the days of my life." Wherever God is—that is where David wanted his home to be. Palace? Great. Beautiful mansion? Marvelous. Mud hut? Perfect, if He is there. But if God's not there, David's not going to be there because he is determined to be always in God's presence. Have you come across that "rather be a doorkeeper" verse everyone likes to quote? This is the same concept, only in different words. "I would rather be a doorkeeper in the house of my God than dwell in the tents of wickedness" (Ps. 84:10, NKJV).

If you consider this seriously, it touches on how you spend or save your money. Personally, I have come to the decision that I will not buy the cozy beach house and set myself up financially so I can just coast the last twenty years of my life in leisure. I have made a decision, even in regard to my finances, that I will not slouch or slumber in my pursuit of the knowledge of God. When I'm seventy-two, I still want to get up at six o'clock in the morning and say, "Jesus, this morning is like any other morning. I hunger for the knowledge of You." Just like David, all the days of my life are going to be spent pursuing my Creator. It's the marathon pace.

To be fair, we must admit that David was far from perfect. He floundered in some serious ways, stepped neck-deep into sin, and made some really bad decisions that had an enormous impact on his life and many generations after him. I used to feel like it wasn't fair that God would bless someone who messed up so badly. He caused a whole assembly of priests to be killed, for goodness' sake—and God still cut him a break! But isn't that really the point? If He did it for David, He will do it for me ... and you.

The key was the constant posture of David's heart. Even though he contradicted God by counting his fighting men, caused a whole group of priests to be killed, slept with a married woman, and set up her husband to be murdered, I guarantee at the end of his life, David's prayer was still the same: *One thing I desire, God ... I want to see You. I want to see and touch the reality of my God.*

Try something with me. Think of a difficult situation in your life. Now disregard the circumstance; forget who was right or wrong, whose feelings were hurt, or who got ripped off. What is the one overarching thing that will still matter in five years? It's that the Lord is always after your heart. How will you react in a certain situation? How will you treat the others involved? What will your heart do? God is always after your heart. That's what the Sermon on the Mount was about, remember? Will you bless, forgive, and intercede? Will you love Him utterly, and love others just as much? David was intent on keeping a steady pace every day he was alive, even when he messed up. He understood that faithfulness was the surest way to be successful in his spiritual journey.

David was convinced that being steady would make his foundation strong, and he knew that encountering the Lord on a daily basis was the only way to fuel the desire to keep pressing on. We see this in the very first psalm as he talks about the person who finds his delight in pursuing God. It even comes with a promise: amazing prosperity is poured out on everything that the righteous touch. When you make the pursuit of God the first priority in your life, you cannot help but prosper under the blessing of the Father.

David wanted to know what God was about, so he meditated on Him day and night. David pursued God to understand His character and peer into the revelation of His nature. He became excited about how God runs His kingdom, which drew him to meditate on God's law. It's a self-perpetuating machine: revelation produces desire, desire produces action, action produces steadfastness, steadfastness brings more revelation.

Many parents have sat down with their child and said, "Okay, after junior high, high school, college, what are you going to do? What school are you going to attend? What will you choose for your major?" But wouldn't it be amazing if they said, "How about pursuing the knowledge of God and how He orchestrates His kingdom? I'm not talking about ministry or becoming a preacher. Now listen to me, because if you do this, I can guarantee you prosperity in the future, regardless of what career path you follow. Put the First Commandment in first place."

You're called to the business world? Pursue the knowledge of God. You're called to be an incredible athlete? Pursue the knowledge of God. You're called to missionary work? Pursue the knowledge of God. Whether you're called to be a musician, a flight attendant, a meteorologist, a plumber, or an artist, as you pursue the knowledge of God, you will prosper in whatever you do. This is the promise of Psalm 1.

THE ETERNAL GASP

Look at the unbelievable encounter John experienced in the fourth chapter of Revelation. This is what I believe David glimpsed. We aren't told that David saw the exact same thing as John (but consider that Moses, Daniel, Isaiah, and Ezekiel all did); however, it is apparent that he saw some things that were more superior than words could express.

Children are fearless and fascinated, constantly asking questions.

A parent doesn't think his or her kid is crazy or ridiculous for seeking answers. On the contrary, a parent bends down to the child's level and responds with true understanding and a smile. Our Father, too, smiles with understanding as we come to Him; He delights in us and in our pursuit. So we're going to ask "what if?" and see where the Lord takes us.

Revelation 4 is not a fictional piece of imagination; it is literal— John was in heaven. John set the scene by describing the very throneroom of God. He then discussed the types of beings in the Lord's presence, finally settling on four wondrous beasts with "eyes in front and in back … full of eyes around and within." Have you ever thought about what they might look like and how they might sound? It has to be incredible! These creatures, looking upon the sovereign God, have eyes around and within. They don't have only two eyes—their body is somehow filled with eyes. They do not rest day or night because what they see is so captivating to every eye and so energizing to their essence. They don't eat, sleep, or get fatigued, and they never look away. Since the first moment of encountering God, they have been praising Him continuously.

Some six hundred years earlier, in Isaiah 6, heaven was opened to Isaiah, and he heard something fantastic: "Holy, holy, holy, is the Lord God Almighty!" And here, heaven was opened again, this time to John, and he heard the same thing: "Holy, holy, holy, is the Lord God Almighty!" We are so content to go about our business in this temporal world while there is a heavenly symphony taking place outside of time. While we all sleep tonight, there's a God, a Creator, upon a throne, and all of eternity is fascinated and captivated by Him! David marveled at the King of Kings on His throne. The twenty-four elders fell down and worshiped Him. The four living creatures never looked away from the beauty of God ...

Meanwhile, dorky Dwayne is concerned about his ministry and whether it will go international. For goodness' sake, who's going to man the phones when it gets that big? What about our careers, our 401(k), and our IRA? What about getting the house we hoped for and whether the hardwood floors in the living room will coordinate with the saltillo tile and the marble countertop in the kitchen? Meanwhile, the people in the Church at large spend most of their time, energy, and money trying to increase their comfort level, their intake of pleasures, and the number of people around them who will give them a condoning pat on their complacent backs.

Beloved, God is waiting to be discovered! He is waiting to be encountered. One of Hosea's big concerns was that his people lost their hunger for the knowledge of God, completely lost their way, and got caught up in the daily grind. And I am committed to seeing a generation awakened to the reality of the Creator—to seeing a generation that will stand before the Lord, regardless of career choice, financial situation, or number of kids, and marvel at Him as they pursue the one thing necessary. I want to see this young adult generation seized with the beauty of God just as the four living creatures were. This is what I am contending for.

Do you ever wonder, when God made these creatures and they awoke, what their first actual thought was? Was it joy, reverence, or apprehension? We do know that when they looked upon this magnificent God, their very core was captured, and they gasped—and that gasp has never stopped. Day and night, they look upon the epitome of beauty, with splendor and majesty breaking forth from the center of His being, and they are eternally overwhelmed. These twenty-four elders and four living creatures never cease gazing at this beautiful God; they are always struggling to catch their breath in the presence of the divine One who fills eternity.

Throughout the book of Revelation, John struggled to accurately describe what he was seeing. As you read some of it, you get the feeling that he's not quite satisfied with his description of this spectacular realm. But in these verses he painted a vivid picture of the creatures' reaction to seeing God. Everyone who sees the Lord like this reacts in the same way. A cry erupts from within them, "Holy, holy, holy, is the Lord God, the Creator of the universe! There is no one else like Him! He alone is the beautiful one!" And I think David had the slightest glimpse of this beautiful God who evokes an eternal symphony that fills heaven. Why do you think he personally funded 288 musicians to lead worship around the clock in front of the Ark of the Covenant (1 Chron. 25:7)?

Revelation and desire touched David, and the only thing he wanted was to pursue God and bless the people of God by compelling them in this pursuit as well. He said, *Let me tell you, when the Holy Spirit opens things up for me and I begin to peer into the mysteries of God, I just want to stand there and behold His beauty!* There is no program in the church today that can reveal the beauty of God to the human heart, and there is no theological doctrine that can express the heart's longing for the revelation of God.

David is not outlining a ten-step teaching on the attributes of God as much as his heart is overflowing from the place of passionate encounter. How else can you explain the way he connects holiness and beauty (Ps. 29:2 and 96:9)? Who among us would have connected those two things on their own? Most Christians think holiness is about resigning yourself to a boring life because so-called fun is off-limits. Not David. He encountered the beauty of God and found that a life of holiness was a posture of worship, a natural response to seeing the Lord as He truly is. He said, *God is so beautiful; I must have more! I want to behold this One all the time. Why would I even want to look away?* Worship just poured from within David—just like it did from the four living creatures who could not take their eyes off God. I think it's from these experiences that David was able to write the psalms.

THE TREASURE OF ENCOUNTER

David had an intimate understanding of God that allowed him to make some amazing statements. It's easy for anyone to collect information from several sources and turn it into his or her "opinion." You just cut and paste, add water, print it, and you're a bona fide authority. But declaring from a place of understanding or experience is a whole new deal.

I say this with a heavy heart, but if we were to ask the average believer to write a paragraph on the knowledge of God—what He is like, His nature, His power, His infinite abilities—specifically from a place of experience and encounter, I think we would be surprised at our inability to articulate and describe God in the slightest way.

You may protest, "Who can really describe God?" Well, John, the writer of Revelation, sure seemed to be able to. Isaiah and Jeremiah did as well. And Solomon. And don't forget Jesus, David, Paul, and Moses, just to name the easy ones. But notice that it was all because they encountered Him. Imagine asking them how God sounds. Like mighty, rushing waters, like a lion striding in all its strength, and a multitude of voices. Well, how do they know? Because they saw Him. And how does He smell? Like myrrh and vinegar, the heart of a cedar tree, and the fire of love. How do they know? Because He called them close to Him. And He is calling you as well.

I think David had intimate encounters with God that allowed him to write things like Psalm 96. An individual who has pursued God in no more than a blasé, nonchalant, dispassionate way cannot write or live in the reality of Psalm 96. Once again, David was overcome by the Lord's glory and wonders.

> *"Honor and majesty are before Him; strength*
> *and beauty are in His sanctuary."*
> *—Psalm 96:6, NKJV*

I think David saw God because he said, *When you look upon Him in His sanctuary, you'll never question if our God has the ability to move creation; He's unbelievably strong. Our God is not a wimp. Strength exudes from His being. The beauty of His sanctuary will overwhelm every sense you've got. He's amazing! He's unbelievable!* You get the sense that David has been there. I think David saw His strength and beauty. I think David touched God. He could only write a psalm like this from a place of encounter and experience.

We must understand that the greatest treasure is waiting in front of every believer. We've all seen reality shows. I'd even guess that you have imagined winning a million dollars. You may not have phrased it exactly like this, but the question comes down to, "What would it be like to have success in this life?" Your definition of success depends on where your imagination has taken you. But whatever definition of success you've formed is only the beginning of what it means to encounter God. A million dollars? A hundred million? All that is nothing compared to experiencing God.

Success looks different today than it did when I was a teenager. I used to want the coolest lunchbox or the nicest jeans, and later I wanted the coolest car. Now my thoughts about success have to do with apprehending God. And believe me, I'll get some little blessings here and there, some small touches on my heart, and all it will do is reinforce my decision to pursue Him in a greater measure. To me, it's imperative that this generation sets their hearts to pursuing God because success comes as we seek Him first.

This journey that we're on is no cakewalk. It requires resolute decisions and then action to see them through because the enemy will go to any measure to keep you from going after God. The enemy will hinder you through pain; he will allow offense to arise within your heart that will color your pursuit, causing you to become a self-centered individual. He will even give you success if it will derail your heart. I'm not at all saying success is wrong in your career, but if you're not steady in your pursuit of God, if you don't have first things first by God's definition, success will dilute your focus and cause you to stray from your initial commitment.

David's example is unmistakable. He said, *All the days of my life, I am going to focus on pursuing this God, so that at the end of the day, I will be found as one who is welcoming back Jesus with my eyes clear, full of light and love, and focused on eternity.* This age ends with the Spirit and the bride saying, "Come, Jesus, I miss You. Come back, Jesus, I want to be with You." And those who set their heart on the same pursuit as David will, in that hour, find themselves crying out in concert with the rest of His people.

STILL FOUND BEHOLDING

At IHOP-KC we hold a few passages very dear in regard to the place of prayer. Luke 11 and Luke 18 are two examples. If we make revival in Kansas City and breakthrough in this nation two of our goals and give ourselves to the place of intercession, we will surely get what we ask for because those verses tell us, *If you stay persistent, the Lord will break in speedily.* So I believe we're going to have change in Kansas City—there's no doubt in my mind.

Another foundational verse is: "That I may ... inquire in His temple" (Ps. 27:4, NKJV). Breakthrough will come someday in Kansas City, but if our end goal is just to see revival, ten years down the road this city will be in worse shape than it was before revival broke out. On the other hand, if one morning we wake up to see people flooding churches all across this city with the sole purpose of encountering Jesus, that prayer meeting will go from five thousand to three hundred thousand! The Church will only get hotter and grow stronger in this land because we will never fully outlive or exhaust discovering the knowledge of God. So we agree with the heart cry of David: *beholding Your beauty is my utmost and eternal call!*

As I labor in the place of intercession, even after revival comes, I will still be found in the place of pursuit and prayer because my highest ambition all along was to behold His beauty, not just to have a limited touch of God upon the city. If now, before revival, I cultivate a heart of hunger and pursue encounter, I will fall madly in love with God rather than quit the ministry again like that time in Budapest. Revival breaking out, signs and wonders, divine power openly displayed—and I, dorky Dwayne, am still there with one thing burning on my heart: *God, I love You so much*. That's how I want to be when the time comes.

I am looking for a generation that is awakened to the Creator, driven by a holy resolve, and entering into fasting and a lifestyle of prayer because of their hunger within. That generation will not be swept away, but will understand their prophetic destiny. And rather than compromise, a righteous hunger and a divine longing will take place within the Church.

We are not going to be a people given to the ease of this life, but rather a generation that hungers and longs to encounter God face to face. We will be a people of holy resolve. There will be a spiritual violence within us—we will contend. We will be steadfast, hungering for God until He splits the sky, until we have an open heaven over this nation, until the revivals of old come once again.

Yes, it'll be fun. Wheelchairs emptied, cancer healed, blindness a thing of the past. But I'm in love with Jesus in the midst of revival because I know He is my exceedingly great reward—I'll be happy with that. This, my dear friend, is the passion worth pursuing all the days of your life. This is truly how it is supposed to be.

THE
CALL
TO
PURSUIT

03

TWO HEROES

I have two heroes who leave me completely astonished and amazed as I look at their lives in Scripture—King David and the Apostle Paul. Their lives were wisely founded upon the pursuit of the one thing. I think of the things they encountered, all the hardships, the attacks of the enemy, and the sheer weight of their own brokenness—yet their stories couldn't have turned out better or more divine. From staring at sheep to becoming king of Israel, God's beloved nation, and from functioning as a legalistic, spiritual dictator (ahem, murderer) to becoming a tender father of every Christian since his time, what was in the heart of these men who desired something singular through every season of life?

In the beginning of Philippians, Paul said a few things that are hard to hear, but they show his heart and the struggle that apparently plagued him for no short amount of time. He discussed his two main desires as a human being and as a spiritual being: to stay and finish his work or to be with Christ. Paul knew he was to walk out his calling, but he said it would be far better to be with Christ. He desired to fulfill the glorious calling set before him, while simultaneously yearning to be with his glorious Lord; he was drawn to stay and to go. This is the tension that beset his soul. Is it possible that he found a way to be with Jesus and still be here on earth? Is it possible that he made Jesus his one thing while still walking the path laid out before him? I believe so, and I think he unveiled his plan in chapter 3. Torn between two desires, he found a way to both encounter Jesus and work as though nothing would fulfill him more.

Every hero has defining moments. They experience historic times that will forever be regarded with honor and pride by those holding them as heroes. A child looks back at his father assembling his first bike, or her mother getting the sticky pink wad of bubblegum out of her hair, or the policeman rescuing Fluffy from the highest branch. A Red Sox fan will reminisce about the 2004 World Series. America will forever remember the service and courage of the firefighters on September 11, 2001. To me, Philippians 3 is one of those defining moments in the life of one of my great heroes.

PERFECT PEDIGREE TRASHED

Paul started by saying he had already spoken to the Philippians about the topic he was about to bring up again. *Guys, I know*

I've talked to you about it before, but please, as you read on, don't take it as a tedious chore. This is foundational ... that's why I'm focusing on it again. And if you have this reality settled within you, I guarantee you will finish the Christian race well. You may not be rich, but I tell you, as much as you set your heart on this course, you will be eternally safe. He knew these people; he knew they would be tempted to tune him out quickly if they thought he was merely repeating his teachings.

I imagine that receiving a promise like this from Paul would have the church on the edge of their seats in suspense. "What in the world is he going to talk to us about?" they probably wondered. He told them not to be stuck on themselves, but if they wanted to compare their status, they were welcome to step into the ring with him. He was guaranteed to win. It would be Godzilla versus Bambi before the deer could stand. We're talking three seconds, max. Then he unloaded his verbal arsenal on them: His parents lived by the letter of the law; his ancestry was elite; he was a true patriot to his country; he devoutly adhered to God's law; he fiercely defended the purity of his religion even to the point of persecuting his own; he was a meticulous observer of everything set down in the Lord's rules—a radical perfectionist on every level, and really good at it, too.

Paul's words don't have the same effect on us today as they had on his audience then. They knew the importance of the eighth day after birth and what it meant to be "of the stock of Israel." But nowadays the average reader's eyes fly past these lines, overlooking some serious name-dropping and prestige. We just don't feel the weight of it, so I want to look a little closer for a moment.

Paul was more or less giving his pedigree. If we were to bring them into today's context, he would be saying that his success had been inevitable. *I was born into the right family—rich, influential, nice people. My education is secure. I was valedictorian in high school, and I'm on my way to any Ivy League school—wherever I want. I have no problems; I'm healthy, wealthy, wise, and charming. I have it all.* He didn't stop there. *I can have any job in North America. Doctor, lawyer, surgeon, mathematician, computer scientist, nuclear physicist ... nothing is too hard for me. I have the brains, the abilities, and the discipline needed to succeed. Yeah, you heard me right. I'm all that and a bag of chips. If anyone has a reason to be arrogant, it's me.* After presenting his worth and potential and outward advantages, and making them all feel like losers in the process, Paul made a dramatic U-turn. He said, *But people of Philippi, everything I can point to and everything that appears so important is truthfully insignificant compared to encountering Christ.*

> *"Yet indeed I also count all things loss for the excellence of the knowledge of Christ Jesus my Lord, for whom I have suffered the loss of all things, and count them as rubbish, that I may gain Christ." —Philippians 3:8, NKJV*

COMPARED TO THE EXCELLENCE OF JESUS

The believers Paul was addressing knew all about his past, how he had hunted down other Christians and publicly persecuted them, oftentimes killing them as he did Stephen. They also knew of his miraculous salvation experience.

Since he was a child, Paul's future had been set, and his influence was undeniable—everyone supported him, and the leadership loved him. And then one day, he was traveling with a bunch of buddies, just enjoying the day, when something profound happened that dramatically changed the course of his life: a Man brighter than the sun knocked him to the ground, blinded him for a season, and opened the eyes of his heart. The Man, Jesus Christ, encountered Paul on the road to Damascus.

Through this dramatic meeting, a deep conviction was birthed inside Paul: it is all loss, all garbage, compared to encountering the Son of Man. These words of Paul practically groan with longing, *Oh, to have the Lord!* He had been arrested with a tangible desire to touch the Son of Man. Paul had truly encountered his exceedingly great reward. No longer did he desire to be honored in the eyes of the Pharisees; no longer did he concern himself with managing his influence; no longer did he vacillate about choosing Harvard over Yale. His arrogance had been crushed, and he found his life to be futility apart from this One who had found him.

Paul said, *Church of Philippi, I want you to consider something. Take everything you want—your future, your goals, your objectives, your talents, everything—and line it up on one side. On the other side, put only one thing: the Man Christ Jesus. Then take a step back and ask yourself some questions. What is valuable? Which is worthy of your pursuit? Do you want to put your energy into your own lofty goals and objectives that will fade in a matter of years, or into this Man, Christ Jesus?*

> *"And be found in Him, not having my own*
> *righteousness, which is from the law, but*
> *that which is through faith in Christ, the*
> *righteousness which is from God by faith;*
> *that I may know Him ..." —Philippians 3:9-10,*
> *NKJV*

I PRESS ON

*"Not that I have already attained, or am
already perfected; but I press on, that I may
lay hold of that for which Christ Jesus has also
laid hold of me." — Philippians 3:12, NKJV*

Paul wanted them to recall the zeal that had driven him to persecute the Church. Now he was focusing that same zeal on encountering this Man. If anything got in the way, he pressed through. Jesus came after him, and now he was pressing on to attain that for which God laid hold of him.

Obviously the statement "that for which Christ Jesus has also laid hold of me" encompasses more than the human heart going after God. We are talking about the Apostle Paul, the man who turned the known world upside-down, preaching Jesus with true spiritual authority, power, and wonders. But that same apostle declared that there was only one thing he really lived for. His ultimate desire and goal was to be in the presence of Jesus, living his life in passionate pursuit of Him alone.

This is the guy who laid the foundation of the early Church. This is the guy who traveled and was shipwrecked, jailed in almost every city he entered, attacked by animals, and beaten time after time. Yet he was tenacious in his pursuit. He said, *My longing and my desire is to be with Jesus; this is what I want. I want the Son of Man in all His splendor. I want the Son of Man in all His glory. I will not let anything hinder me—not other pleasures, not finances, not depression, not death. I will let nothing hinder me from encountering Him. I will press on.*

"Brethren, I do not count myself to have

apprehended; but one thing I do, forgetting
those things which are behind and reaching
forward to those things which are ahead."
—*Philippians 3:13, NKJV*

At first glance, this may not mean a whole lot, but consider who the Apostle Paul was ... a murderer, and not just your accidental blue-collar killer either. As an ultra-Pharisee, Paul (then called Saul), had made it his life's mission to hunt down, persecute, and kill faithful believers. He had been persecuting and condemning the very people he finally turned to run with. Paul actually participated in the murders of those who followed the Man he himself fell in love with. You want to talk about shame? You want to talk about brokenness? A first-degree murderer was saying these words: *Forgetting who I am, I press on. I press on so that I may know Him. When I encountered Him, He wiped my slate clean. Shame does not control me now. Nothing will hinder me from Him. I press toward the prize of having Christ Jesus.* I love this.

I have seen many who have let their past derail their future, who believe they are discounted for this reason or that. I am not minimizing anyone's past. I know many people intimately who have horrendous pasts. But if God is committed to releasing revelation to you and encountering you, will you choose to disqualify yourself (even though He doesn't) to the point that you will not pursue Jesus or let Him come near you? Samson, Zacchaeus, David, the thief on the cross, or any of the disciples had good reason to give up, but none of them did; instead, they all chose to stay in the running even though they made huge mistakes. Like Paul, they said, *I will press through everything to encounter Jesus. Yes, I have both done and endured some atrocious things, but I will not allow those things to lock my heart. I will not allow my past to keep me from touching the Son of Man.*

Bad things happen to everyone. The only difference is whether you allow those things to separate you from God, or whether, like Paul, you resolve to let nothing hinder you from encountering this Man, Jesus. Will you believe that His delight is still on you, that He still enjoys you, that He really likes you? If so, it will allow you to "press toward the goal for the prize of the upward call of God in Christ Jesus" (Phil. 3:14, NKJV).

THE CALL FOR YOUR GAZE

On your journey as a believer, questions automatically arise. Who am I and what is my calling? Am I called to be a deacon? Am I called to be a pastor? Am I called to be an evangelist, a fireman, or a retail salesperson? Am I called into counseling, sports medicine, or intercession? Paul lets us know that those questions are good starting points for a young believer, but as you mature in your faith, the callings that once consumed you begin to diminish, and the supreme calling to one thing becomes ever clearer. Whether you are anointed or not is no longer the motivating drive of a mature individual. The motivating passion becomes: Am I tender toward the Lord? Am I moved when He comes near me? Instead of being consumed with numbers and results, ask yourself: Do I hunger for Him like I used to? Is my gaze still focused and are my eyes pure? Is my heart expanding in the understanding of this Man, Jesus? Paul's exhortation is clear. As you mature in faith, your pursuit of Jesus becomes more and more consuming.

People look at disruptions in their lives and cannot comprehend what God is doing to them. There are all sorts of thoughts that can take over. *God has left me ... Why has He left me in this place? I feel so alone ... I guess I pushed Him away with my sin ... I'm in a desert season ...* I've heard them all. Honestly, I think the majority of the time, God brings disruption because He is hungry for your gaze. God knows that if He gets your gaze, even if it's due to confusion or loneliness, He will get you. Disruptions, though confusing to the human heart, are needed because they compel us to look upward and concentrate on Him for a season.

I am even tempted to think about what happened on September 11th. On a national scale, one of the big questions was, "Where is God?" Unquestionably, the Lord was not distant and removed. He earnestly desired the gaze of this nation. What does it take to catch the eyes of a nation that is saturated with darkness, wandering aimlessly, and headed straight off a cliff? Is He willing to bring disruption to arrest the heart and the gaze of a people? This should not seem odd. Consider the loving parent who sees his child headed toward certain heartbreak, irreversible emotional damage, or physical danger. Would he not do whatever possible to rescue his beloved child? Then why should we expect anything less from the epitome of love?

THE CALL TO YOUR FIRST LOVE

When I was asked to lead Onething, IHOP-KC's young adult conferences, I spent a lot of time asking God questions. "Jesus, I want to know what the condition of the Church is today. Specifically, what is the condition of the young adult community? How is their heart before You? What does it look like?"

As I was reading the book of Revelation, I came across the first letter to the church in Ephesus, which is found in chapter 2. The Lord gave them a commendation, a rebuke, and then a solemn charge. After first affirming their commitment and focus, He hit them with a double whammy: they had lost their first love and their tenderness. When His name was spoken, their hearts were not moved anymore. When they lifted their eyes in worship, desire was not there. So the Lord lifted His voice: *I call you back! I was the One who won you, and I want your gaze; I want your heart back, and I want your focus to be completely on Me. Yes, you have a commitment to the Church, a commitment to labor, and a commitment to proper doctrine, but I tell you, there is something more. I want your whole heart, and I want it tender.* I think a large portion of the Church would find themselves in this place today.

The second passage that stuck out to me was Revelation 3:15-16. "I know your works, that you are neither cold nor hot. I could wish you were cold or hot. So then, because you are lukewarm, and neither cold nor hot, I will vomit you out of My mouth" (NKJV). It pains my heart to say this, but I believe many churches in the United States are in this position, not meaning to hurt the Lord's heart, but doing it nonetheless. They say, "Life is great. Our congregation is growing; we went from five hundred members to six thousand in five years. Life can't get much better than this. We have need of nothing."

Yet heaven has a slightly different take on things. "Because you say, 'I am rich, have become wealthy, and have need of nothing'—and do not know that you are wretched, miserable, poor, blind, and naked—I counsel you to buy from Me gold refined in the fire, that you may be rich; and white garments, that you may be clothed, that the shame of your nakedness may not be revealed; and anoint your eyes with eye salve, that you may see" (Rev. 3:17-18, NKJV).

My personal opinion is that September 11th was a wake-up call to the Church in the Western world, a little heart-prick from heaven. I believe that God was saying, *I want you to know that the way you perceive yourselves is different from what I think of you. I call you back from the lukewarm state, from the heart that is full of mixture and compromise. I call you back to My heart. Come back to Me.* I love verse 19 because you get a glimpse of the eternal Savior's heart. He says, "As many as I love, I rebuke and chasten" (NKJV).

He is committed to capturing our whole heart, no matter what it takes. He is committed to capturing the gaze of the North American church. He wants a lovesick bride. And He will seek her attention in one of two ways. First, He gives her the opportunity to voluntarily pursue Him with passion and love. She receives the invitation to get herself out of the muck and the mire, out of all those things that have entangled her so that she can break free and run with passion after God. If she does not voluntarily respond to the Lord's wooing, He will try a second way to win the fascination of her heart: chastening and rebuke. He says, *I love you. I am committed to you. I am committed to getting your gaze because I am a jealous lover. I will not have My Church pursuing any other loves, but I will get you to return to Me, full of passion, either by awakening you with revelation or by putting roadblocks in your way.*

In Philippians 3:15, Paul said that maturity is about your heart being alive in Him, and that the Lord is absolutely committed to revealing it to you even if you don't understand it all yet. All you have to do is position yourself by doing what you already know you should do. He then gave more hints: *Church in Philippi, you have seen my passion and my hunger for this Man, Jesus. I am calling you to the same one thing—love the Lord and pursue encounter. Join in following my example and the example of others who do the same. This will keep your heart alive with passion. If you don't, you will become like those I've talked about before, and now tell you about with weeping, who are enemies of Jesus.*

This is the part that I have spent a great amount of prayer on. You can almost feel Paul asking, *Remember those who used to run with us? Remember those who used to call on the name of Jesus? They were with us in the meetings. They would pray and worship with us.* I can see him even writing this letter—tears in his eyes—and saying, *I tell you with weeping, there are those who used to run this race with us who are actually now enemies of Jesus—enemies of the cross.*

Consider the condition of North America today, and those who once lived within the boundaries of the Church. These people pursued the "church program"; they pursued cultural Christianity. Yet many of them are now losing their way because they were only attendees. As soon as they walk away from any type of structure and their faith falls apart, it becomes obvious that there was no foundation or root system in the reality Paul urged the Church to have. Many have placed their hope in the Church, yet the Church is stumbling. So Paul said, *Get your gaze back on this glorious Man; He will sustain you, He will keep you safe, He will keep you from wandering, He will keep you strong in even the darkest hour.*

Remember, Paul repeated himself to his friends on purpose. He wasn't worried about sticking to the scheduled lesson plan for the month, nor was he worried that his congregation would recognize the message. Remember his words: *For me to write these things to you is not tedious, but safe. Please, Church of Philippi—please, Church of North America—you will be safe and secure if you find your reality in this. Remember, there is no confidence in the flesh. In fact, count all things loss. Just throw it all in a biologically hazardous waste bag—for the excellence of the knowledge of Jesus. If you count it all as rubbish, you will gain Christ.*

Paul had divine revelation from heaven. The Son of Man had encountered Paul, and Paul's eyes were blinded and then opened again. He had insight on these things. He knew the human heart and the things that distract it—even good things, like a prestigious pedigree. And Paul was weeping. He was left broken by the reality that many have become enemies of the cross. With great pain in his heart, he was saying that these followers, these cell group members, these pastors and missionaries, these disciplers and Sunday school teachers will one day be enemies of the cross. Paul's warning was, *They have no true religion, and they will perish in the same manner as all sinners. A mere profession of faith is not going to save them. Their end is destruction.* For this type of person, Paul said, their god is their belly. They worship their own appetites and live not to adore and honor God, but to gratify and indulge themselves.

The crazy thing about the belly is that you feed it, and less than six hours later, it comes back at you with intense hunger. If you do not feed it something of substance, it is always hungry. Have you ever heard that if you just keep on nibbling, you will never really be satisfied, never really get full, but will always feel hungry? That is what Paul was saying here. The Philippians never grasped the true divine substance, so they began to allow the natural tendency toward self-indulgence to drive them.

His next phrase is "whose glory is in their shame—who set their mind on earthly things" (Phil. 3:19, NKJV). They indulged in modes of living that ought to have covered them with confusion and brought shame, but instead they lived it up and gloried in it, showing it off like a trophy. Pursuing the pleasures of this life had overrun them, and they were chasing after worthless things with all their heart, mind, and soul. Seeing the heights they fell from should have brought a sting to their heart, but they felt no loss, no shame, no remorse.

My perception is that many in this generation, sitting in their stiff pew, have come to the conclusion that things are not fulfilling them—the message didn't come alive within them. I can almost feel the swaying hearts of a people who have yet to feel the passion they read about. I can almost hear the groan of the common Christian on Sunday morning, "Wait, the sermon is over? I came hungry, and I'm leaving hungry. I have not touched something of substance that moves my heart today."

The heart is massively hungry, much more so than the stomach, and it will move an individual to make a choice—either life or death. The human heart has longings and cravings; if it is not set on the right thing, it will take you down the wrong road.

My conclusion is that many are sitting within the boundaries of the Church today, driven by their appetite for something of substance. Their heart is hungry, their longing true and profound. Yet they have not been pointed in a direction that might satisfy, nor have they been given something that would sustain them. And they have gotten themselves into a place where their pleasures and pursuits are of an earthly nature, which ultimately will not satisfy the human heart.

Because they can't deny this hunger and longing innate to every human—this longing for something of substance and reality—

they've begun to set themselves on the "American dream," on just maintaining their cultural Christianity, on the car, the house, the career ... and it tricks them. They begin to think, *Oh, it's not really that bad; it's not evil.* But as we commit to the overwhelming mortgage, the loan on the car, the children and their three music lessons per week, slowly we lose our main pursuit. Honestly, the pursuits of many in this culture are so unfulfilling. What they are caught up with, what they are scrounge around for, and what they get excited about is so inconsequential, not only now but in the light of eternity as well.

So many have bought into this culture and the pursuits of this society hook, line, and sinker, and they are totally bored. The hunger doesn't go away; the longing doesn't disappear—it just finds new ways to resurface. And with all the stimulation that is offered, it's easy to find a new "thing" each month until you are overloaded and bored with life at the same time—overloaded with what's available, bored with every last ounce of it. Something has to be fundamentally wrong if you give yourself totally to something and it still leaves you wanting. Paul said, *Many who used to run hard after Christ with us have chosen a life outside of the One who called them. They are eating of pleasures that satisfy for only a season; their glory is in things of confusion, and they are covered in shame and brokenness. They have set their mind on earthly pleasures that matter and satisfy for only a season, and they have lost sight of their true reward— the exceedingly great reward of having God Himself.*

Your youthful zeal is powerful. The hunger of the human heart, when it is combined with this human zeal, is incredibly powerful. But if they are not channeled the right way, on a marathon pace, you will find yourself heading down the wrong road—whose end is not found with Jesus.

I am sure you can say, "I have friends who used to run with me, but they no longer do." I believe it's incredibly simple, if you were to boil it down, why this happened: they never truly touched Him. They never found that they could buy into this Man, Jesus. The Bible calls us to a marathon pace, not a two-minute sprint. It is a lifetime pursuit. But many get into it and run the race for only a short season. I mean, they haven't even scratched the surface of who this Man is, yet they say, "It didn't work for me. It didn't quite meet me where I needed it to." But they are the ones who never took His offer seriously and never truly touched Him.

Looking back at the words of Paul, we can see that he's trying to get us to understand something: when you said "yes" to Jesus, you said "yes" to a totally different kingdom, set of values, and set of pursuits. You said "yes" to pursue a King who is not of this world. You are no longer to sit and look at your neighbor's house and compare it with yours, because the sum of your life is bigger than what you acquire.

Paul said, *Today, I am calling you away from the lesser values of your society and culture. I am calling you to walk as I have walked—in my shoes, in my pursuits, in my goals. Because, at the end of the day, your eyes will be clear, your life will be focused, you will be found longing, and your heart will be hungry for an encounter.*

WERE YOU ABLE TO LOVE ME?

Once when I was standing before the Lord in prayer, I saw a person from China, a person from Africa, and me ... the bald guy. Jesus looked at the individual from China and said, "In all My sovereign wisdom, My decision was for you to be born and raised in China. With all of the problems, persecution, and discomfort, were you able to love Me?"

Then Jesus looked over at the one from Africa and said, "In all My sovereign wisdom, I chose for you to be born in the midst of Africa. It is AIDS-stricken, poor, torn by violence, and oppressed. In the midst of those circumstances, were you able to love Me?"

Finally, He turned to look at me. "Dwayne, in all My sovereign wisdom, I chose for you to be born in one of the most affluent societies on the globe—the height of pleasure, entertainment, wealth, and worldly pursuit. In the midst of all those pursuits, were you able to love Me?"

Talk about a shock! I immediately thought, *That is what it will be like at the judgment.* At the end of the day, on the scale of life and death and eternity, the pleasures and pursuits of the society that we live in are nothing. Yet we are surrounded and consumed by them; they saturate us. In this culture, we are taught to pursue success—to aim high—and we have fully bought into the entire façade of this culture. The kicker is that we all know it's fake, a sham, a vanishing charade—the Matrix, if you will. It's not real, in an eternal sense, but it is definitely all around us, endlessly bombarding us.

The real question for each one of us is: has the grand illusion of this culture stolen my gaze? I do not want all these things that surround me to hold such a place in my life that they may actually take away from my opportunity one day to stand and say, "Jesus, I said 'no' to everything—everything that got in the way of You. I said 'no' to everything holding me back from a heart that would be moved at the very mention of Your name." As Paul reminded us, *You are not supposed to live according to any value that would come in contradiction to the value of pursuing Him.*

I carry a deep conviction that, within this nation, there will be a day your faith is tested. I believe a day will come when the Church will be tested with greatness unto martyrdom. There are massive numbers of believers, even today, who are constantly tested in their faith ... just not in North America yet. If those who are being tested have set their hearts on pleasures that will last only a fleeting moment, they will crumble under the test of persecution. But Paul said, *I want the Church strong and confident. I call you to get your gaze on this glorious Man, so that in the hour of pressure, in the hour of testing, you will stand strong because your gaze and your eyes are focused on Him.*

There is great pain in the Church today. Many are wounded; many are wandering; many have lost their way. But one experience with this Man, Jesus, will change your life for eternity. One experience with Him will leave you captivated, longing for more of His presence. The call within my heart for the Church today is a call to the First Commandment. All my heart, all of my possessions, all of my energy, all of my soul, and all of my resources need to be focused on this Man. There is to be a tangible tenderness in my heart toward Him. I am to love. I am to weep. I am to be passionate unto Jesus, and everything else will fall in line. I am calling you back to the First Commandment—to fall in love first and foremost—that you would truly love with all of your heart. Are you able to love Him?

There is a glorious hour coming to the Church. I pray, labor, and fight for the anointing of the Holy Spirit across this nation. A day is coming when a twenty-two-year-old woman will walk up to a person who has no hope left—a cancer-ridden body with only days to live—and lay hands on that person, praying, "Jesus, I ask today that Your power would be manifested in this cancer-ridden body." And the sick person will arise, instantly healed. That is where I believe we are going as a Church. That is what I labor and fight for—preaching with power and authority like John Wesley, Charles Finney, George Whitefield, Smith Wigglesworth, and Jonathan Edwards. I am fighting for anointed preachers to arise within this generation. And what is going to get us there is a heart without compromise—not worried about the crowds, the anointing, the money, the numbers, the next conference, but about the tenderness of your heart toward Jesus.

We need to ask one question: is my heart fascinated with this glorious Man? And when we have hundreds of thousands who can answer "yes" to this question, who love Jesus unto death, and who are willing to lay down their lives, the glorious One sitting on His throne will say, "I have a trusted Church to whom I will give My power without measure." That Church will arise lovesick, preaching with apostolic power, as thousands come to the Lord in one day. That's what this is about—a glorious Church that loves Jesus and is moving with apostolic power. So I call you to love. I call you to pursue Jesus. This is the greater joy and greater call that awaits us.

One day this glorious Man is coming back. One day the sky will split and Jesus will appear. And do you know who He is going to find? A people who are lovesick, infatuated with Him, without spot or wrinkle—there will be no blemish in that Church. She will be pure in devotion, in love with the Son of Man, willing to lay her life down in a moment, all because she loves. This is what was breaking Paul's heart when he said, *Many have lost their way.* Like Paul, I feel that many in the Church today have lost their way. I want to give them a wake-up call. I want their hunger to be satisfied and their hearts to come alive again. I want them to stand on that glorious day—fascinated and in love.

Jesus, let it be. Jesus, release wisdom and revelation in the knowledge of who You are. Jesus, awaken us this hour; awaken the Church—that we would love, that we would adore, and that we would pursue without compromise.

LOVING
WELL

04

RECOGNIZE WHO IS IN THE HOUSE

"Now it happened as they went that He entered a certain village; and a certain woman named Martha welcomed Him into her house. And she had a sister called Mary, who also sat at Jesus' feet and heard His word. But Martha was distracted with much serving, and she approached Him and said, 'Lord, do You not care that my sister has left me to serve alone? Therefore tell her to help me.'" —Luke 10:38-40, NKJV

Looking Martha in the eye, Jesus focused in and gave her His attention. He said, *Martha, you are worried and troubled about many things. These things are beginning to consume so much that you cannot see who is standing in front of you.* Then He pointed over to Mary, her sister, and said, *Your sister has chosen the good thing to be consumed with, the good part of life. Mary has chosen something that will never be taken away from her.*

It is unbelievable whom Martha invited into their home. She said to Jesus, *Will You not come in? Bring Your disciples too; I want you all in my house. Please come in.* Right away, her sister recognized who Jesus was. If you look at the context of the story (and keep in mind the culture at that time), you will find that Mary, seated among Jesus and His disciples, was not exactly in the proper place for a woman. In those days it was not appropriate for a woman to be sitting and receiving from a teacher—especially from a rabbi. However, Mary knew who was in the house that day and sat at His feet with an adoring gaze.

Mary clued in right away—a chord struck within her, and she would let nothing hinder her from sitting at the feet of God in the flesh. He touched her deep within, and she was greatly moved. This Man sparked a tenacious zeal within her, and she didn't care about breaking the customs and courtesies of her day. Her response was, *I do not care what others may think about me; I will be found at His feet. I would do anything to get near this Man because I understand the richness of the One sitting in front of me.* So she found herself at the feet of this houseguest, Jesus.

Martha, however, had not yet clued in to the amazing gift of His presence in her house. God Himself was present, but she didn't get it. This Man was like no one else in all creation, yet Martha was unable to understand His identity. Jesus said, *Distraction has consumed you to the point that you are unable to see who is standing in front of you. Your eyes are blinded; you are unable to recognize the identity of the One in your house.*

Think about what an amazing experience it would have been to have the eternal Man on your sofa. What would you give to have Him come and sit in front of you just so you could be at His feet and hear the words of life? Yet Martha was completely distracted and unable to see the very One she loved.

Many believers have said, "Yes, I will give You everything because I want You," but it would do us good to keep it in the forefront of our understanding as we walk out this life. When you said "yes" to Jesus, you put a massive bull's eye on yourself. Right then, the enemy committed to destroy any passion and love for this Man you have given your heart to. The enemy's main goal is to steal, kill, and destroy you. He intends to steal affection from the Son of Man. He is plotting to send any distraction your way that will derail, demotivate, or cause you to slow down. When you waiver, wonder, and allow his lies to affect your heart, he begins to win the battle for your passion. Ultimately, it is not about your time or how you spend your money. It is about something much deeper. Does your heart move toward Jesus?

BLINDING DISTRACTIONS

Distractions come in many colors, and they are tailor-made to attract your gaze. Success could be your biggest distraction. The entire North American culture is geared around success, and in the end, pursuit of success will be the downfall of many believers. When you live for success, you will get it if you pursue it hard enough. But in the hour of your "achieved success," you will be so filled with your dreams, with managing your life, bank account, honor, and power, it will blind you and leave you incapable of having room in your life to desire Jesus. When this happens, the enemy has succeeded enormously.

Pain can also be a big distraction. How many times have you heard this story? "I found a great church and loved it for the first year. Then I had a bad encounter with a certain leader and ended up being hurt. I was incredibly wounded by the church through that experience, and it has left me in great pain." When this happens, the enemy has succeeded enormously.

Even when terrible things happen, a believer can arise in the strength of the Spirit and say, "I am not going to camp out here, because there is a glorious One waiting for me to encounter Him. I simply cannot and will not let the pain of my relationship with my family, the pain from my local church, the mistreatment from trusted friends, all the wounds and injustice—I will not let these things rule me. No, there is a glorious Man waiting for me to seek Him out and touch Him. I have my eye on something greater than this world. Yes, I have been incredibly wounded. Yes, it was unjust. A family member has victimized me. A loved one has cheated on me. A trusted leader has betrayed me. I have been lied to, and I have been judged. Yes, it was unfair and wrong, but this is not who I am, and I am not going to live in this place. I refuse to spend my life as a victim. I want to know Jesus more than I want to remain a victim. I will not let pain rule me." In that place, passion and zeal for the Son of Man prevail, and the enemy has failed to steal your gaze.

Even religion can serve as a distraction. As a nation, religion is more like a baby pacifier than an encounter with God. Pacifiers quiet, calm, and socially compose because no one enjoys a screaming baby. But the real thing (milk) is given to satisfy hunger. At church, you could easily sit there and feel like you are doing as the Scripture instructs. However, the reality is that nothing is moving within your heart; often you are not having your hunger satisfied. It does not take long to realize that filling a space in a building reserved for religious activity is only a pacifier, while your true cry is for something of substance.

Let me give an example from a recent speaking engagement at a secular university campus. I was interested to see what was going on within that type of atmosphere, so I asked a few questions. I found out there were about twenty thousand attending the university. I asked the staff how many students would call themselves Christians. Between 60 and 70 percent. After hearing that I asked, "Now tell me, how many actually love Jesus to the point that they order their life around Him?" Their answer: around 10 to 12 percent ... maybe 15 percent at the most. They couldn't give hard numbers, but that was an educated guess.

It was difficult to get up before the student body to speak. With so many calling themselves Christians, it was harder than I thought it would be. *My goodness*, I thought, *this is like walking through mud.* It was hard to preach, just like back in Budapest, and when I gave the altar call at the end, only about ten people raised their hands. I said, "Okay, let's pray," and the whole audience bowed their heads in prayer. To put it lightly, I was shocked. At the most, I thought the ten who raised their hands would sheepishly bow their heads while the rest would just stare at me. No, everyone in the whole audience bowed their heads; they simply knew that was what they were supposed to do. The religious spirit was ingrained; at that moment they were not pursuing divine encounter, but rehearsing a religious act, dutifully observing religious protocol. Before I could think it

LOVING WELL

through, I asked this question into the booming microphone: "Do you guys understand what you just did? I called you to prayer and you knew what to do. But nothing moved you on the heart level. It was merely tradition, the outward appearance of praying." They were unable to understand, but Jesus was waiting to encounter their hearts.

So many have bought into this "I'm okay" religious lifestyle, yet on the inside they are screaming and longing for eternity to move them. They are simply stuck in a religious structure that cannot move them an inch closer to the Son of Man. The enemy has blinded so many believers in this nation. Many have bought into a religious lifestyle—the pursuit of success, raising their children to be moral citizens, saying prayers before meals, attending church regularly, and maintaining a happy—even victorious—life. However, they are not moving any closer to understanding the heart of Jesus.

Hosea said that when we lose the knowledge of God, we will lose our way (Hosea 4:6). Nothing of the Son of Man is being preached on Sunday mornings in many congregations, and it is hindering a greater measure of encounter with Jesus. In most places today it is all about attaining a lifestyle and acquiring more—it's the consumer-driven church. It's more along the lines of motivational speaking with a scripture as a reference. Where does that leave us? Many in the Church today are hungering and longing for something of truth and depth, but leadership only offers them a pacifier. The enemy is also bombarding us with distraction. Even the religious lifestyle numbs us to the reality of Christ Jesus.

I know that failure has been a major source of distraction for many. We've all heard the hurtful words that judge us as a failure. "You are never going to make it ... You're not good enough ... You're not smart enough ... You can't sing that well ... Your ideas aren't that great ... It'll never work." In that place, the enemy keeps tripping you and tripping you and tripping you, and you end up losing hope and heart. Slowly you give up and begin responding from a wounded heart. You say, "I have tried this road before, and it just did not work. I keep failing and going backward."

When speaking about failure, one of the things Mike Bickle mentions is the groups of people with whom he has been in connection over the years. "There have been three to four different groups of people who have run with me—one when I was fifteen to twenty years old, another when I was twenty to twenty-five years old, and another when I was twenty-five to thirty-five. Today, if I turn around to look for them, I find they are no longer there. Instead I see that some of their marriages are a mess, they are in crisis mode all the time, and they are depressed and spiritually disoriented. I am not calling them to a life of ministry. I have called people all my life to a lifelong pursuit of the knowledge of God to a heart of going after Jesus. They have given up because they say it was too hard. Do you know why it is too hard? Because it is impossible to manage the culture of the hour and also manage a heart for the Son of Man. You cannot have both. You have to have one or the other. You cannot buy into the culture of the hour—those paradigms and those pursuits—and also buy into loving and pursuing Jesus the way the First Commandment says."

BEWILDERMENT AND DISILLUSIONMENT

Jennifer and I were driving the other night when I brought up a pretty big subject. "I want our kids to have a great work ethic. When they agree to something, regardless of what it is, I want them to follow it through."

Have you noticed that, on average, young adults within this nation do not know how to stick with something? They do it for about a month and then say, "I tried that, but it's not exciting anymore." Then disillusionment sets in because they tasted something, but never really stuck with it. They never really pursued something of substance that they could hold on to and cultivate.

An easy example is relationships. You discover an attraction to someone and pursue this person for a little while, but it somehow grows old. Regardless of the reasons, you quit. And this translates into the statistics of marriage. The marriage starts out great, but again it's cut and run after a little while. Believe me, I know it can be a lot more complex, but the numbers don't lie. The divorce rate is astronomical—more than 50 percent, in fact, depending on whether it's your first, second, or third marriage (*www.divorcestatistics.org* shows the rate going from 45 to 73 percent, respectively). You can't possibly say that half of all marriages "just didn't work out"; there are deeper issues here. Maybe it's a bit more inflexibility than incompatibility. There are growing stages in life, but you have to push through so you can come out with something of substance on the other side. This is the reality of life.

What about a college major? How many friends have switched three, four, or five times because it wasn't as thrilling once they got into it? And what about a job? How many have they had in the past two years? During the Depression no one squabbled over what kind of job they had; they were simply overjoyed if they had one. Not so nowadays. How many times have you heard, or said, "It needs to match my personality ... and if it doesn't feel right in a few weeks or a month, I'll find something else"?

This flawed approach is seen on a daily basis throughout the nation. I think we need to have our understanding of this life recalibrated to a marathon pace. Microwaves only work for food; everything else takes the same amount of energy, but requires more time.

A certain posture of the heart (often called diligence, faithfulness, or patient perseverance) will allow me to push through, so that at the end of my days, my passion will have only increased since my youth. As age increases, I may become a bit slower in my movements, but my zeal will only grow in its strength and hunger. That is my lifelong pursuit. At the end of each day, I want to say, "Yes, you can take everything away, but you cannot have this hunger and this longing I have for Jesus." It will be my one thing eternally.

THE MODEL OR THE MAN?

I believe spiritual hunger is at an all-time high in this nation, but the Church is not meeting that hunger with anything of substance. It seems there is a massive crisis, and the leadership of the hour is even beginning to speak up. I am reading a book right now, and the author concluded, "Either I write this book and lose all my friends, or I can continue to live this life and despise my own reflection every morning." He obviously decided to write the book, and in it he says the program we currently call "church" is not working.

According to a 2005 study by Barna, five out of six people pray every day; six out of ten worship every day; 82 percent of Americans call themselves Christian; and 84 percent of that number say they live a (ahem) simple lifestyle. Between you and me, does that include the plasma TV, the game console, and the money spent on entertainment? In 2004, only 4 percent of American Christians tithed on a regular basis. Eighty-two percent believe they're fine with God, but where people spend their money is a reflection of where their hearts truly are. For argument's sake, let's look at the 4 percent as truly pursuing God. Of this number, the exodus from the Church as a whole is at an all-time high.

The February 2005 issue of *Charisma* Magazine published some statistics about people leaving the Church. The numbers were unprecedented. Right now, those who are fifty-five years and older are paying the bills for the Church; 80 percent of the Church's income is attributed to that demographic. So if we continue on this current path, the emerging generation will find itself in true chaos. The financial pressure will cause many in church leadership to preach messages intended to keep people in the pews—messages of prosperity, the American Dream, and victorious living—to the detriment of a life spent in pursuit of Jesus.

This may hurt your feelings a bit, but Jesus did not call us to the American Dream. In fact, at the end of the day I am called to give up every distraction that would hinder me from living out the First Commandment with intensity. That's not to say that we should spend our lives aiming to be unsuccessful underachievers, but we should ask ourselves these questions: Have we bought into the American Dream and forsaken our true spiritual inheritance? At what cost will we compromise? Do we sell our soul for cheap?

In another ten to fifteen years, the entire landscape of the North

American Church will be radically changed. Some have already noticed this and are trying to figure out new ways to do church. Model after model has popped up, each with its benefits and hindrances. We are starting to see church differently and find new ways to bring forth its best aspects. This is the key: models will differ, often out of necessity, but preaching truth will sustain the heart (for instance, preaching about Jesus Christ and eternity). Because North American culture changes, church culture changes, and it forces the model to change. However, the model is not the issue. The message is.

The church model has changed significantly in the last thirty years, and it will change several more times in the next twenty. We went from the average congregation to the megachurch to the small group model to having the seeker-sensitive plasma TV screen or meeting in unconventional locations. Twentysomethings have experienced the plasma-screen television church service, only to notice that there is nothing of depth to move them—not because the new models are wrong necessarily, but because there is simply a lack of divine encounter on a daily basis. And this is true of any model that does not center on becoming God's.

Although it's natural for church culture to change, we have changed church structure due to ulterior motives. We realize that people are hungry, so we think that changing the model will feed them, instead of realizing that we need to lead them to Jesus. Changing the format of church without offering truth has caused us to lose our way.

Lately we are seeing many twentysomethings who are truly hungry walking out on the whole seeker-sensitive movement. It seems more that the thirtysomething audience has bought into that type of model. Large churches in the seeker-sensitive movement are mostly composed of families still trying to go after that comfortable lifestyle, with nice, comfortable messages and programs to suit their every need—all the while not realizing who is waiting to encounter them.

Christian twentysomethings are now hanging out in bars, using this logic: *Let's just sit, have a drink (because we're not religious), be cool, and talk about Jesus. In that way we will say we are looking after the poor because that's what Jesus would do if He were here.* That may last for the next few years, but then another person will come up with another great idea on how to gather people under a new banner. I believe there is a crisis in this land of an unprecedented order: while searching for a new model, we have lost our First Love.

While this may sound incredibly simplistic, I believe part of the reason you may be reading this book is that the message of Jesus satisfies a hunger within you. This call is not to a movement, a religious structure, a fad, a specific model, or a single person. It is a call to a Man, to Christ Jesus. When He said, "I am the bread of life," it meant that only Jesus satisfies the spiritual hunger within you—not a cultural setting, a church building, or a group of people. Only when I touch Jesus is my hunger satisfied.

It does not matter how you do church. Do church however you want, whatever it looks like, however big or small. But if you talk about Jesus, His resurrection, His power, and who He is as the Son of Man, that is what will satisfy. That honest approach will spark interest, and individuals will come and begin to partake of this One.

We must understand that He truly is the Tree of Life and that when we partake of Him, we are fed within our spirit. I may not have food to eat, ten pairs of black shoes, or extra money to toss in a wishing well, but I tell you, I am alive on the inside. Whatever church model you want to go after, do it. Just put Jesus at the center of it, and you will have life forevermore.

You want to build a church? Call the congregation to the Son of Man; instruct them on the excellencies of this One. When we do not preach Jesus on platforms or describe His excellencies, we are not fascinating or winning over the human heart; we fail to grip it with a surpassing awe and an eternal gasp.

DIVIDED PURSUIT

I believe that when God created me, He put within me a foundational part of DNA: I was made to be awed, fascinated, and exhilarated. The human heart was made to be exhilarated, and it is all about the Man sitting on His throne—the One who has captivated eternity. Whenever human eyes have seen Him, they have been captivated over and over again.

A heart that is not fascinated or won over will pursue anything to be moved, therefore making it ripe for the seeds of compromise to be planted. This can lead to a heart divided in its pursuit, prohibiting someone from being able to sustain anything in a wholehearted way. When compromise begins to set in, you no longer have the energy to continue your first priority and your first pursuit. Ultimately, then, you find yourself in the same boat as the church of Laodicea.

The Laodicean church received an incredibly strong rebuke from Jesus: *I would rather spit you out of My mouth. I do not want you in My presence, because you are neither hot nor cold. I would much rather deal with you in rebellion because I could quickly bring conviction and clearly show you where you are wrong.*

I love how Jesus ends His interaction with that church. He said, *Your heart is mixed in its pursuits, but I am the God of love. Therefore, because I desire you, I will chasten you. I am committed to getting your gaze, so I am going to chasten you with the least amount of discipline; all I want is your heart fully given over to Me in love.*

Right now, I truly fear for this nation and for this generation because I know He is willing to come in with judgment and discipline to get the hearts of the Church. September 11th was a road bump, a little test, and I do not believe the response was appropriate for what the Lord was doing. America filled its church pews for a season, but we went straight back to our overloaded lives and distracting pursuits. Nothing really changed in our hearts concerning our pursuit of Jesus.

I think we in America are living in a very serious hour. Many are saying crisis is coming—and if our response to this crisis is anything less than calling people back to Jesus as their First Love, this nation is in trouble.

Warren Buffet is one of the richest men in the United States, but he has pulled all of his money out of the U.S. dollar. He refuses to trade it because of its instability. Argentina's financial situation is dire—the entire nation is bankrupt. Many are saying that one slight movement in our economy will cause the United States to end up just like Argentina. There are probably at least ten similar scenarios, but it boils down to the fact that this whole nation is built on a house of cards. One movement, one shifting, one little upset could bring down the whole house.

You can feel instability in the air—we are in such a fragile state. And if we do not understand that any shaking that comes our way is intended to turn our love and passion toward the Son of Man, we are going to find ourselves in a difficult place— humbled by the hand of the divine God. More than anything, He wants the complete love of our hearts.

In 1 John 2:15, John said, "Do not love the world or the things in the world. If anyone loves the world, the love of the Father is not in him" (NKJV). He pointed out that it is easy to figure out where your heart is. If you buy into the cultural norms of the hour, your ability to love the triune God will disappear. It really is simple—your desire and longing will not be there.

John said, *I want you to consider something. Please, just listen and take heed of what I tell you. I'm not trying to keep anything good from you, but trying to keep you from trouble. I'm not trying to make your life boring or void of pleasure—exactly the opposite. Do not love this world, please. Do not buy into its values or cultural norms.*

The danger is to look at your neighbors, the Johnsons, and see their lifestyles and pursuits. Often the social status, the pristine reputation, the impressive education is because they want to give their children every opportunity they missed out on in their youth. This is the pursuit they have bought into. Yes, every parent wants to give good gifts to their children. But the right school for the perfect resumé for the someday-prestigious position is not the ultimate gift.

John beseeched us not to buy into that. He said, *Do not set your house up in such a manner that a perfect earthly career and reputation are what you live for. If you live like that, at the end of your life, when you stand before Him, your heart will not be inflamed with passion and longing. When you buy into the cultural norms of the day, you will not be able to have passion that will move you to the One for whom you were created.*

We are not to make this world the object of our affection or the anchor of our hope. We are not to be influenced by the trends and feelings that prevail this hour. The one who gives himself to the things of this world will not long for Jesus.

My goal in sharing this with you is to give you something more than basic mental assent, beyond the *Yeah, yeah, I know He's God and stuff*. My desire is that there would be an awakened hunger within you—that there would actually be a longing to be in Him and to say, "Jesus, I desire You and You alone! It is my heart's cry to encounter You. That is what I am living for! I am living for a person who moves me like nothing else could. So I will abandon everything that hinders me. Distractions will be removed because I have an ache for You, Jesus! I have a longing and a hunger to be with You! I desire You and You alone!"

Our ability to love is truly limited because we are finite people. The human heart only has so much affection, and it is physically impossible to have two lovers as number one in your life. John said that when you give yourself to other loves, you will not be able to find your way. Having inflamed passion for the Son of Man has to be your heart's singular cry.

When His name is mentioned, I want something to happen on the inside. I want my heart to respond and be so moved by longing that I give up other fleeting pursuits that look worthwhile and legitimate to my earthly mind.

If you are not moving forward in your pursuit of God, if you are not continually taking new ground within your own heart and spiritual life, you are actually losing ground. If there is nothing motivating you on a continual basis, you will find yourself slowly drifting back.

Have you ever noticed how it is always the eighteen-year-olds who can't wait to go on the missions trip? They are the ones who can't wait to do the extreme and the wild. Of course, I think some of it is their stage of life and amount of energy. As those eighteen-year-olds journey into their late twenties, when it comes to their willingness to sacrifice in order to experience a greater pleasure, the momentum and the movement have weakened. I have seen many drift backward. At that point, no longer pressing on for an encounter, they are vulnerable to disillusionment and distractions that may consume their hearts.

THE OFFERING OF YOUR LIFE

As He stood in front of her distracted sister, Jesus looked at Mary and touched the central issue in the heart of every human being. What was that issue? At the end of our life when we stand before Him, He is going to grade each of us on only one thing: did you have a zealous love for Him that motivated you all the days of your life?

Jesus said, *Mary has chosen to posture her heart the correct way, and she is giving it her all.* Then—I love this—He said that desire would never be stolen from her. This same thing applies to us today: only one thing is needed, only one thing is necessary. As you begin to live that out, everything can be taken from you, but the longing of love can never be stolen if it is continually fanned into flame.

From the mouth of Jesus came the truth that one thing is necessary, and, like Jesus promised Mary, that desire and longing will never be stolen. This heart posture is what the Son of Man is looking for from you. He was not joking when He said all of the commandments were wrapped up in this one reality.

When you decide how to spend your money, does it pass through the paradigm of, *Do I love the Son of Man?* When you spend your time, is it aligned and in accordance with, *Do I love the Son of Man?* When you spend your mental capacities in reading books, studying, and interacting intellectually, does it go through the filter of, *Do I love the Son of Man?*

Jesus wants you to have a passion that aligns your finances, your time, your strength—everything—with the reality of a heart leaning into love. Look at Mary. She had this posture. And this is what He is calling you to.

So when I stand before the Son of Man, I want to have eyes that are clear and focused. I want to be able to say, "Jesus, I loved You well all the days of my life." I want to be able to lift my hands and say, "What I have done I offer to You. But what I have most treasured is my desire for You—and I give You my love. Jesus, I loved You well all the days of my life." If I cannot say that, I will be incredibly disappointed, and I will have failed. By today's standards, if I have nothing in my bank account and can't point to a recent promotion, it looks like I have failed. But that is not what heaven says. The Lord knows my weakness and immaturity, but He sees my longing, and it makes Him move toward me. That is success.

In Mark 14 we find an amazing story about Mary of Bethany. "And being in Bethany at the house of Simon the leper, as [Jesus] sat at the table, a woman came having an alabaster flask of very costly oil of spikenard. Then she broke the flask and poured it on His head" (Mark 14:3, NKJV). This flask of perfume cost was incredibly costly. She must have spent all of her life savings on it, yet she poured it out on Jesus' feet with pleasure, expressing her devotion. Her actions declared, *Jesus, this is all I have, but I want to pour it out in complete devotion to and desire for You. It costs me everything to love You, and I do it gladly.*

> *"But there were some who were indignant among themselves, and said, 'Why was this fragrant oil wasted? For it might have been sold for more than three hundred denarii and given to the poor.' And they criticized her sharply. But Jesus said, 'Let her alone. Why do you trouble her? She has done a good work for Me. For you have the poor with you always, and whenever you wish you may do them good; but Me you do not have always. She has done what she could. She has come beforehand to anoint My body for burial. Assuredly, I say to you, wherever this gospel is preached in the whole world, what this woman has done will also be told as a memorial to her.'" —Mark 14:4-9, NKJV*

Jesus was using Mary's heart as the model of desire and devotion. He lifted her up as the example. He said, *This is what I am calling you to. This is the model of devotion and love—a heart that is willing to give up everything and lay it at the feet of God.* She is the model of the life we are called to lead.

There is only One who can satisfy my longing. So I seek Him, though it costs me everything. I am giving up all I have and all I am because I long to gaze on Him. My prayer is, *Jesus, I will give my all to something, somewhere, and I want it to be You. What else is worth devoting my life to? It is You I want and nothing else. So I offer You everything I have. You have moved me, You have won my heart, and I want to give You everything.*

If you do not have this hunger, I would question whether you have even touched Him. If you have heard the Gospel preached in such a manner that you are not wounded by His love, I wonder if you have really heard the Gospel. Mary was one who truly encountered. She knew Him.

Mary said, *You guys do not get it. I touched Him; He has wooed me and stirred me. This is what motivates me. This love is the longing that drives me. I will pour over Jesus every ounce of love. He has touched me, and my response is to give everything. I will lay it all at His feet because I have been stricken with love.*

My fear is that the Church today has not heard a true message of Jesus. When I look at the condition of the Church, I see very few signs of true encounter. From that we can deduce that the true Gospel has not been preached. More often than not, we have been given a dog-and-pony show. Have we not simply been told what we wanted to hear? Haven't we been thoroughly entertained?

Sadly, however they win us over, they have to continually feed us in order to keep us coming back. If they teach a message on a victorious life (how to succeed, live a better life, get more, become great, be happy, overcome, and take your promised land), they will have to continue to preach similar messages, so as not to rock the boat. In this environment, messages on brokenness, spiritual depravity, sacrifice, simple living, and utter humility won't pack out the congregation and bring in the big tithe checks.

If you prioritize a victorious life over pursuing love, the pressure that will inevitably come will overwhelm you. In that time of stress, you will buckle at the knees and give up, without understanding why life is so difficult. If you have heard about the beauty of Jesus and the gospel of love, which cause shame to break off your life, your eyes and heart will be full of Jesus, and you will be an overcomer.

If the Church would preach on the excellencies of this Man, the true message of Jesus—His undeniable character, the fullness of His emotions, His rapturous affections, His overflowing heart, His tenacious pursuit—then when the sermons stop and the hour of testing comes, the wounded people in the Church will be strong—not in their own perceived greatness and success, but in the strength of the Lord. In that hour they will say, "Take anything you want, but you cannot have my love. It cannot be stolen. It is the most precious thing I have, and I do not care if I have anything else. I desire Jesus; desire is what moves me, motivates me, and keeps me standing. I am not living for this life; I am living for Him. Take whatever you want—I am His and He is mine."

Even at a place like IHOP where prayer and worship never stop, we can sometimes fool ourselves. Even though I call myself an "intercessory missionary," I can still become so absorbed in my other responsibilities and pursuits that I find my motivations were not from Him. Yet, I can fool myself into thinking I am doing well because the job is going well, because the results are more positive than negative.

Regardless of the subculture you are in, I want to call you to a passion that moves you unto the heart of Mary. Regardless of your career path, I want to call you to utter longing, to a heart that is moved by love as you seek after Jesus Christ.

The enemy has blinded many in the Church in North America with endless distractions. We are so consumed that we are unable to see who is standing in front of us, inviting us into the depths of eternal love. We may be consumed with success or failure, or with the stresses and responsibilities of normal life, or maybe with keeping up with the extravagance of the neighbors. Managing the culture of the hour while simultaneously cultivating an inflamed heart for the Son of Man is a spiritual impossibility. You cannot buy into the culture of the hour—those paradigms and those pursuits—and also buy into loving and pursuing Jesus the way the First Commandment says.

Many have bought into the religious lifestyle that numbs us to the reality of Jesus' existence without moving us any closer to understanding the heart of Jesus. Many in the Church today are hungering and longing for something of truth and depth, but leadership only offers them a pacifier. Slowly we begin to give up and respond from a wounded heart that has yet to be fully restored.

Thankfully, the structure of religion was never meant to satisfy; Jesus alone satisfies the hunger within you. The Gospel is a call to a Man, Christ Jesus, not a cultural setting, a church building, a specific ministry model, or a group of people. Only when you touch Jesus is your hunger satisfied. As you see Jesus, desire will be awakened within you—a desire that can never be taken away—and you will offer your life to the Lord as one who has loved well. The passionate "yes" in our hearts will ravish Him, and He will invite us into His eternal embrace as a faithful and fully pleasing bride, the delight of His heart.

A JOURNEY WORTH TAKING

05

LOVE BEGAN IN GOD

Pursuit. Though many of us desire to pursue God, most people simply don't know how. What is it that takes our passionate "yes" and sustains it for the long haul, from start to finish? Obstacles, detours, and traps catch us off guard, causing our hearts to waiver and our pursuits to become hindered. In facing the harsh realities that are out to ensnare the human soul, there is a key to sustaining the heart that longs to go after God.

Even within the Church, many are missing it. Many are sitting in their pew asking an ever-present question: why do I go to church anyway? *Yes, I believe in God. Yes, I want to live for God. Yes, I want to be a Christian ... yet something is missing.* To those, I say, "Yes, there is another way to live." There is a reality beyond gritting your teeth and bearing it, or going through the motions of "church" for the sake of social perceptions and self-imposed duty. The key to sustaining a passionate life within the wall of the church is to have a heart that is passionately in love with Jesus. There is a deep pleasure, a sustaining zeal, and a fiery passion available—and they are only found within a life of intimacy, an abiding love relationship with Jesus.

We all like to say we have a relationship with God, but where did the idea come from and why do we need it so badly? Relationship is central to every human being. That's one reason why solitary confinement is such an impacting punishment and why neglect leaves such a devastating emotional scar on the soul. The study of anthropology has shown that relationship is one of the basic needs of every human being. It is the foundation of our very existence—we were created for relationship. Yet, even in the Christian community, many have not experienced or touched the kind of relationship we were designed for ... and they are therefore struggling to live the life in God they long for. The relationship He created for us is founded upon tenderness and longing—His tenderness and longing for us. The key to passionate pursuit hinges on understanding this.

The whole idea and emotion of love actually began within the heart of God. "Love is of God ... for God is love" (1 John 4:7-8, NKJV). Love began in God; it is the core of what constitutes His existence. Just think about that. The concept of affection and desire is of God, and it is important that we root ourselves in this understanding because it leads us to the deep things of His heart. This speaks massively of His disposition (the way

God operates and the way He approaches His creation). For instance, how does the Lord interact with people? Does He stay at a distance like an apathetic husband who busies himself with work, or is desire the very essence of His heart? Beloved, love is of God! He is a lover. I think this first understanding is probably the most significant step in our journey.

Let's take that step right now by exploring a biblical concept called the "Bridal Paradigm." It sees Christ as the eternal Bridegroom and His people as His bride. It's a way of viewing God and His interaction with humans through the relational lens of intimacy, like a marriage. You've heard the adage about the Bible being a love letter from God, right? Well, it couldn't be truer.

The Bible begins with a wedding between the first man and woman, Adam and Eve. Sprinkled throughout Scripture is example upon example of bridal imagery—Hosea and Gomer, Ruth and Boaz, wedding parables, and even the Last Supper. The Bible ends with a Spirit-empowered bride singing the eternal wedding song as we welcome our Bridegroom's reign (Rev. 22:17). Jesus is the Bridegroom, and we the Church are His bride. Everything He does overflows from His heart of love.

As God interacted with the nation of Israel in the Old Testament, many times He approached her as her Husband; He committed Himself to her at such a deep level that only the language of union could touch upon His true feelings. So everything that you find in the heart of a bridegroom toward a bride, you will also find in the heart of Jesus toward the redeemed—delight, enjoyment, passion, affection, desire. Jesus, the Bridegroom, pursues us at the deepest and most intimate level of relationship possible—that of a husband toward his wife.

Just to be clear, gentlemen, this has nothing to do with you walking down an aisle in a white dress or some weird sexual identity thing. I'm a guy, and I can't feel for Jesus like that. Jesus is simply communicating on the deepest level possible. It has to do with the most intimate of relationships, the way God sees you, and the identity we will have in the eternal age. He will forever be our Bridegroom; we will forever be His bride.

The Bridal Paradigm is crucial for every believer to understand because if you do not know the motivation of His heart, you will often be tempted to question Him and His leadership in your life. On the other hand, if you realize that every movement of His heart happens because He wants you, you will more readily align yourself with Him regardless of what He is doing. If, at the end of the day, you are completely convinced that every decision He makes in regard to you is based out of His intense desire for you, you will align yourself with it. If you do not know that, you will resist God and His moving in your life. I'm not talking about throwing up your hands in bitter resignation or making Him drag you, kicking and screaming, along the (ahem) glorious path of life, or saying a bunch of positive statements you're not sure you really believe in the deepest corners of your heart. I am talking about diving into every situation of your life as His partner because something deep inside of you knows He is a lover and that everything He does fosters that love.

> *"He who does not love does not know God, for God is love." —1 John 4:8, NKJV*

For you to truly love, you must experience the God of love. For you to truly have affection for a sibling, friend, or spouse, you must first encounter the God of love. It's the concept of "like begets like." Affection begets affection. Tenderness begets tenderness. God begets love.

I love my middle daughter, Chloe, but I want to love her more, so I go to the source. I need to spend time before God and let Him tell me what He thinks of me and what He thinks of her. I need to touch the very affections of the Creator. Once I catch the smallest glimpse of His emotions and feel what He feels toward Chloe and me, I am able to truly love through the glimpse I just received. I can turn around, look at Chloe, and say, "Sweetheart—oh, you are so wonderful!" I can say it because I have just received it, because the heart of God has just overwhelmed me.

We must be convinced of His nature and His disposition. God begins to extend His hand, and when I feel Him reaching toward me, it makes me want to move toward Him. His is not frustrating, apathetic, impatient, cold, distant, sterile, or unmoved. At the very core of His being, He defines Himself as love. At the very core of His being, He defines Himself as affection. At the very core of His being, He defines Himself as tender, as delighted in me, as excited to see me. When I begin to see this, it makes me want to go to Him. As I have said before, when I see that He completely delights in me every moment of the day, it causes me to love Him that much more.

LIES OF THE ACCUSER

In the book of Revelation, we see that we have an enemy who stands before God's throne. His main endeavor is summed up in the name the Lord gives him: "the accuser of the brethren." He is seen as a beast and a dragon as well, but in regard to his function concerning the saints, he is seen as an accuser. The picture is rather simple, and its power lies in a comparison: Jesus is at God's right hand interceding for us every moment of the day; Satan stands before the throne, attempting to separate humans and God every moment of the day.

His accusations take on several forms. The first is to bring a charge to God about you. He basically says we're bad, based on the legal grounds of our sin. "They sinned, so they deserve punishment. You're just, so You should be the One punishing them. Why don't You whip out a lightning bolt and get to work?"

The second is when he speaks lies to our hearts about the character and motivation of God's heart. The accuser of the brethren is constantly challenging your knowledge of God's heart. He will tell you that God is frustrated with you and disappointed in you. He taunts, "When will you finally stop messing everything up? You realize He can never truly like you until you straighten up, right?" In dealing with our shortcomings, most of us are under the impression that the Lord is impatient with the slow rate of our spiritual growth and that our sins have totally isolated us from Him. If we stay on that path, eventually we end up believing that our weaknesses define who we are rather than trusting that His heart defines us. But when you understand that at God's very core is deep longing and that, regardless of what you do, His longing is still pursuing you, those misconceptions begin to break down.

The point is that God is not distant from you. He is not frustrated with you. He is not impatient, but He is constantly pursuing you and is filled with delight and desire for you.

Please hear me. I am not saying that sin is okay—no way, not in a million years—or that God just looks the other way so you can do whatever you want. What I am saying is that He knows the difference between your immaturity and your rebellion. Throughout Scripture we see the wrath of God manifesting in various ways. But each time, He gives plenty of room before He drops the hammer. You may recall this notable sentence in the Bible: "If they will return to Me, I will relent."

The repentant heart, though stuck in sin, always turns around, saying, "I wish I never would have done that!" If that is your heart's cry, the eternal Bridegroom is waiting to encounter you. Your repentant heart can encounter, touch, and experience the God of deep love—always. It has to do with the condition of your heart. The rebellious heart will encounter the wrath of God, but the repentant heart will be enveloped in His love. A measure of discipline and correcting may be part of that encounter, but discipline is very different from wrath. The discipline of God stems from love, and its purpose is always to enhance love. Wrath is given to the rebellious; discipline is for the enhancement of affection toward the Son of Man. He says, *I want everything removed from your heart that hinders you from touching Me. You may need to have your life shaken, disciplined, or disrupted, but it is to enhance the pursuit of the repentant.*

God's wrath does not come to those with an earnest "yes" in their hearts. And my guess is you are reading this book because you hunger, because you appreciate conviction in your heart, and primarily because you want to touch this God of desire and affection.

THE GOD CALLED LOVE

> *"Beloved, let us love one another, for love is of God; and everyone who loves is born of God and knows God. He who does not love does*

not know God, for God is love. In this the love
of God was manifested toward us, that God
has sent His only begotten Son into the world,
that we might live through Him. In this is love,
not that we loved God, but that He loved us ...
Beloved, if God so loved us, we also ought to
love one another." —1 John 4:7-11, NKJV

Love is the necessary foundation for carrying out the First Commandment, followed closely by the Second Commandment. We can only love God if we understand His love for us, and we can only love one another if we first understand His love for them. The natural overflow of a heart that has touched God is to love your neighbor as yourself. When you love God, He gives you compassion and tenderness for your neighbor, your family, your spouse, your friends, your enemies, the lost ... for everyone, really. For those who have touched this God of love, their love becomes mature and perfected.

On your journey, it is necessary to understand the nature and character of this God who calls Himself Love. As the body of Christ, it is essential to operate from a place of transformation through the emotions and affections of Jesus. That is a hefty statement, so I'll say it another way: once we have been touched by His love, we are transformed and can start living from that perspective. We can truly say that we know and believe the love God has for us. We have experienced Him, and now we are convinced. We have been transformed by love, and we will never turn away.

As John, known as the beloved disciple, expressed, *I have touched Him. I have experienced this One, and I am completely convinced that nothing can steal away God's love for me. My heart will never be shaken from this reality. Death, success, poverty—nothing can take away this desire. Everything is shaking, everything is being challenged, everything is being disrupted in my life, and I have lost everything—but I am 100 percent convinced: God loves me! I will never walk away!* I can just feel the passion John must have had as he looked back on the short yet profound time he spent with Jesus. He had actually tested the boundaries and felt the Lord's desire for him in every circumstance.

Try to shake that picture of John as a wise old man out of your head—it's just not true. He was still a young guy when he joined Jesus. All of them were twentysomethings. I guarantee these twelve were dorky and immature. Imagine Jesus looking around and saying, *Who do I want as the founders of My kingdom?* He looked to the religious establishment of the day. *No, that will never work,* he said. *But look over there at that twenty-two-year-old mechanic—I want him!* And that is who He chose. Out of the entire world and all its inhabitants, the young and immature twentysomethings are the ones He sought.

Looking back, John said, *Remember us? We were young and immature. We stumbled and fell often, but we landed softly. We tested His nature, His tenderness, and His desire toward us. We tested all of it every time we stumbled and fell. We were sure He would be gone when we turned around, but instead we found that He was leaning into us. Hey, Peter and James, remember when we would fail? And what it was like to look into those eyes? I have never forgotten that gaze. Now, as a mature believer in the faith, I can say I truly believe the heart of Jesus toward me. I am totally convinced that there is a foundation into which I have been rooted—the love of God, which knows no height, no length, no breadth, no width, no end.*

I believe this is why those young apostles could stand before their accusers. It wasn't because they had youthful zeal or because they were incredibly boisterous or strong. No, they could stand against whatever the enemy brought against them because, at the end of the day, they knew they would get to be with Jesus. Remember Paul saying his heart was torn in his letter to the Philippians? He knew he was supposed to be here, but his desire was to be with the Lord.

Fear did not hold the young apostles back from their destiny. The Bible says, "There is no fear in love; but perfect love casts out fear, because fear involves torment. But he who fears has not been made perfect in love" (1 John 4:18, NKJV).

This is a profound verse for those who struggle with fear. I look at this in two different ways. First, you may struggle with many fears in your own mind: fear of death, fear of the future, fear of losing your job, or fear of the unknown. These are simple fears based on uncertainties and a lack of spiritual maturity—they come from not knowing God as well as you should. But as you mature in the journey and come to know the peace of God, these fears will lose their grip on your heart. Secondly, this truth affects people in regard to the fear of man—and God has really been stretching me in this way. As the foundation of my life becomes rooted in God's heart toward me, I begin to let go of what others think of me. The opinions of others are no longer shaping me; God's opinion matters more than everyone else's. Fear of man allows the opinions of others to matter more than of God. But with "perfect love" we understand how He feels about us and can live as if His opinion were the only one that existed. As love is perfected and matured in us, fear cannot have its way in our lives.

When love matures deep within our souls, man can no longer intimidate, coerce, or move us. No longer is our sense of worth wrapped up in what anyone thinks about us, whether it's good or bad. We find our confidence in the all-surpassing love of Jesus. If we lose it all, if they don't like us, if we're not invited to the party, it is inconsequential. Sure, it would be nice, and we would enjoy it while it lasted, but it doesn't matter. Being grounded in the love of Jesus means fear cannot have its way with us.

JESUS, THE ETERNAL ROMANTIC

Love will never flow from a heart until Jesus awakens it. The Bible says, "We love Him because He first loved us" (1 John 4:19, NKJV). We cannot love without first receiving His love. He has set it up that way, and His plan is divinely perfect. He is the initiator and pursuer of any affection within the human heart. The whole reason believers can stand with their hearts focused on Him is because they have felt His heart toward them.

The journey of a believer is often something like this: "I understand salvation's message: there is nothing I can do to get God to love me so much that He'll save me. He loves me a lot already and proved it by dying on a cross, and my salvation only comes through believing in the cross." So we accept salvation.

Then we take an equation that is deeply embedded into us as human beings, especially in North American culture, and transpose it into our Christian walk. The equation is called success. In North America there is only one way to achieve it, and it looks something like this: I go to school and make honor roll every quarter. My parents get a bumper sticker to prove it. I come out of high school with really good grades. I get into the right university and get really good grades. Then I've got a strong resumé to get in with the right company and make the right connections. Suddenly I have ample opportunity for success. I do my job well and get the promotion. I'm doing great!

But if I hit a couple of bumpy seasons in high school and my grades slip, the university I want to attend is suddenly no longer available. So I take the second best option and flunk out because I didn't really want to be there in the first place. Now fast food becomes my grand career. Unfortunately, I get demoted from cashier to "the guy who adds the extra cheese" because I wasn't good with people. All because I didn't earn that cool bumper sticker for my folks in elementary school.

Now be honest. Don't we usually take this ingrained equation into our relationship with God? It is so easy to have an equation for our life in Him that stems from our equation for success. If we succeed, He likes us; if we fail, we no longer feel His pleasure. Perhaps this sounds familiar: I get saved, go through discipleship, and understand what it means to have a quiet time and not to lust, gossip, or hate. For extra brownie points, I do some accountability stuff with my friends and wear Christian T-shirts to school so everyone knows I really am saved. I do okay for a couple of years, find the love of my life, and get married. We put two "holy mackerels" on the back of our car and make them look like they are kissing so everyone will know we are a happy Christian couple. We fight a little bit. It is okay but not the best.

Bottom line: I flunk out at that, and all you can offer me is a "God loves you" with a shrug that means, "but I really can't figure out why, you loser." Here's my response: "You don't understand where I just came from or what I just went through, do you? Yeah, God loves me, but He loves everyone. Jesus came to show God's love; the Father sacrificed Him to pay for my sins; and now the Lord is stuck with me because He already killed Jesus and He can't take it back, right? I thought that was the way the Gospel worked."

More often than not, this is the understanding we take into our relationship with God. When we feel that we are doing well, we believe He likes us. But if we stumble in sin, we believe we lose His favor and become disqualified. Doing well? He likes me. Doing badly? I guess I no longer have the privilege of feeling God's delight. In my opinion, that viewpoint misses the romance that brims from the heart of Jesus.

When His heart is revealed to you, you will understand how He looks at you and says, "I completely understand your journey, for I walked with you. Remember when you stumbled and fell? It didn't rule you out because I knew what you were going to do when I called you." He has seen your path in life, what you will do, where you will succeed, and when you will fail ... yet, even knowing all of it, He chose you because you are His cherished one. Our emotions and categorization of our good days and bad days are not accurate litmus tests of His eternal love. Whether you stumble or succeed, fail or get honor roll has nothing to do with His affection for you. Quite simply, He wants you—regardless of the state of your life. If you are broken, He wants you. If you're covered in shame, He wants you. If you are confident before Him, He wants you.

All He wants is for you to turn and say "yes," because that is the place of delight for Him. When your heart is focused on Him, He can tell you what He thinks about you. When your heart is postured in such a way that you are looking at Him, He can pour His delight over you and into you. Wouldn't you like to be in a place where you can feel the delight of God washing over you?

I believe this One called Love is anticipating the hour you will turn your gaze toward Him. He is excited because He knows that at the slightest step of faith on your part, He gets to pour into you. So I picture it like this: things are going great; life is good; and all of a sudden there is a little roadblock in my way. I cannot find a job, and my bills are piling up. He has actually placed this little disruption in my journey. Because of that disruption, the average believer says, "I'm going to invest a little more time and energy into praying." As we lift our eyes and say, "Today, I am in need of You," I think the Lord of Heaven rejoices, saying, "I've got his eyes, if only for a season. This is what it's about. This is where I want him. He doesn't fully understand that this has nothing to do with getting a better job or paying the bills; it has to do with Me catching his gaze. I am making his heart hungry and full of longing for Me."

Let's set the record straight. Yes, you are called by Jesus. But this life is not entirely about your ministry or the way the Lord uses you. This journey you are on is not solely about your gifts or calling; at the end of the day, the success and impact of your life are not the issue. This journey is about falling head over heels, madly, and desperately in love with Jesus. It's about taking all of your energy, strength, finances, and time, and aligning them in such a way that your primary pursuit is to touch Jesus. Again, it's called the First Commandment. You only have one short life on earth, one small chance in your eternal history to give your love and your life to Jesus. This is it, and then it's gone. The choices you make mean something to Him. What you do matters. So love Him well, because it's all about love.

DEFINED BY HIS DELIGHT

1 Corinthians 2:7-12 is another passage that has helped me in my journey. But first a few questions for you: What do you believe is in the Lord's heart toward you? Is He mostly disinterested in what happens in your life? Does He not see all the injustices that have come against you? Is He generally mad at you for messing things up like He always knew you would? Or is He somehow smiling with approval and delight over you? You must discover God's heart for yourself, because at the end of the day, your belief of what God thinks about you is what will define you. What God thinks and how He feels about you greatly shape you. Like anything in life, you will have great days and completely horrible days. In those times, the stabilizing factor, the place where you draw your identity from, is what comes out of God's heart toward you. That will never change; rather, it will massively define who you are as an individual.

At the risk of sounding cheesy, this passage has actually been my prayer for you as you go through this book. The first few verses are Paul's testimony of what happened when he visited the church in Corinth. "But we speak the wisdom of God in a mystery, the hidden wisdom which God ordained before the ages for our glory, which none of the rulers of this age knew; for had they known, they would not have crucified the Lord of glory" (1 Cor. 2:7-8, NKJV). Paul was saying that there have been hidden mysteries in the heart of God for ages and ages, but now the Holy Spirit is releasing these bits of wisdom to mankind (also called "the revelation of the knowledge of God"). In verse 8 Paul said that if those men had known they were really crucifying Christ, they never would have done it. But they just could not see it, could not believe it, could not understand God's divine plan. Paul then compared their blindness with an inability to see His goodness. You see, the Holy Spirit is releasing a new revelation of the knowledge of God, but, "as it is written, 'eye has not seen, nor ear heard, nor have entered into the heart of man the things which God has prepared for those who love Him'" (1 Cor. 2:9, NKJV).

Let your imagination roam, and try to articulate this One called God. Go to the highest of your lofty thoughts, as far as you can reach. Go to the ceiling of your imagination, where the best is just not good enough, amazing is lame, and perfect can still be improved upon. That place is only the starting point of this One called God. The mind cannot comprehend Him or what He has in store for those who love Him. You cannot begin to fathom what is out there waiting for those who say "yes" to the journey. To those who have positioned their hearts in love, saying, "I don't understand it all, but I choose Jesus; I desire You," revelation and mystery will begin to be imparted. If you've set your heart toward God, you will learn that He covers all your wounds, fulfills your inner longings, and wants to encounter you in ways over and above what you could ever fathom. No mind can comprehend what awaits the believer.

> *"But God has revealed them to us through His*
> *Spirit. For the Spirit searches all things, yes,*
> *the deep things of God." —1 Corinthians 2:10,*
> *NKJV*

Paul said, *I want you to know that when I speak of this Man, Jesus, it is actually contradictory to the wisdom of this age.* You cannot understand Jesus through any known means like understanding math or gathering information about petunias, cooking a filet mignon, or visiting the Grand Canyon. The Holy Spirit is the only One who can help you understand Jesus, and

He longs to reveal the mystery of Christ to you.

The human mind, which is carnal, cannot figure out what is in the heart of God. Without a renewed mind, without the revelation of the Holy Spirit, you cannot sit down and try to map your life out or figure out what grand things await you. You could not even begin to comprehend His heart. But the Holy Spirit searches the deep things of God; He is eagerly pursuing the knowledge of this God of massive depth and width and height. He searches out the very nature and character of God, imparting the Father's heart to you as you pursue Him.

> *"For what man knows the things of a man*
> *except the spirit of the man which is in him?*
> *Even so no one knows the things of God except*
> *the Spirit of God. Now we have received, not*
> *the spirit of the world, but the Spirit who is*
> *from God, that we might know the things that*
> *have been freely given to us by God."*
> —*1 Corinthians 2:11-12, NKJV*

I don't think this is only an intellectual understanding;, I think this is really about a "heart understanding." It's about knowing in the deepest place within your being. You start out unable to fathom what it will be like when Jesus, the eternal Bridegroom, touches you. But when the Holy Spirit begins to reveal this mystery of the Son of Man and His burning heart, and when that revelation begins to unfold, it touches your core. He comes to the ones who say, "I don't comprehend everything, but what I do know is that I love you, even if it is weak, immature, and clumsy."

I always tell this story because I love Him for this. I walked into IHOP-KC at about 10:30 one night, and I could feel the intensity there. As usual, I sat down, but just as I was opening my Bible, I started to feel His presence. For about thirty minutes I had the deepest and richest dialogue with the God of desire. I came in saying, "I want to know You." I was hungry that night, and He pierced me. I wept and wept with new understanding: *You love me, You love me, You love me!* It was not an intellectual comprehension, but a deep touch inside me.

These encounters with God are defining who I am. Success in business does not define who I am and neither do the numbers at conferences. Jesus telling me He loves me defines who I am. As that begins to be the foundation of our lives, we will all truly be impacted.

The Trinity is a wild thing. I truly wish I could figure it out, but I honestly have no idea how it works. I cannot fathom how They are three, yet truly one. We have these three eternal beings who operate as one, yet Paul told us that the Holy Spirit goes on His own journey and searches out the deep things in the heart of the Father. The Holy Spirit literally finds the hidden mysteries of the Father and the Son, and begins to search out those on earth who have their hearts postured to love. The Holy Spirit gives the invitation, *To those who have a 'yes' in their heart, to those with their heart postured in love, this nugget of truth has been prepared just for you. It doesn't matter whether you are mature or not.* The Holy Spirit finds pleasure in searching out the deep things of God and in revealing them in order to produce a human heart that is fascinated by the Lord.

At a quick reading, you might not find much in verses 11-12, but take another look. Paul said that these mysteries have been given to you for a specific purpose—so you would know them, feel them, and understand them. They would touch you, and you would encounter God. The Holy Spirit reveals these mysteries so they can impact you in a deep way. The purpose of the mystery, the reason the Holy Spirit begins to unveil the One we call Jesus, is so you can understand Him. Paul was inviting us into something astounding—the deepest places of the Godhead, with the Holy Spirit as our tour guide.

This revelation can impact you in such a way that you begin to live differently. The mystery of God is waiting for you to experience it and be energized to continue on your journey. Once discovered, it begins to take root deep within you and pierces your soul, enabling you to stand strong even through the deceptions. These revelations, no matter how small, are meant to have impact; they are meant to fight through the lies that have been built up against the knowledge of God. They are meant to pierce those accusations within you that wrestle with who He is. They stir your heart and slowly change your thinking to align with His.

The Holy Spirit does not reveal Jesus so we can look from a distance with disgruntled desire. Yet, as His Church, we often stand far away and say, "Gosh, isn't God cool? Wouldn't it be great to experience and touch Him? And when revival comes, all our problems will be solved." Then we return to our business, to those things that consume us on a daily basis. Something about that is wrong. The Holy Spirit gives you revelation so you can be awakened in longing and desire. Revelation, the gift of those little mysteries, is not given for you to take and toss aside. It is given to escort you into the depths of God.

When pondering these realities, I like to look at the life of David. He was a little guy that no one really noticed, stuck in the middle of nowhere with some sheep on the back side of a hill. But he was chosen to get a little something of God. When he experienced it, he treated the revelation as a true gift. He cherished the insights given to him, realizing, *Wow, the Holy Spirit actually found this and revealed it to me! Selah.* David treated it as a treasured gift, interacting with it and dialoguing with the Lord about it. It was of incredible value to him. It was his pearl of great value, the hidden treasure of incomparable worth. He then took that revelation as his gift and fed on it. He allowed it to affect him and change his core. It went deep and became the challenging and guiding Scriptures we read today. Through David's reaction to the revelations given to him, I am able to experience what it means to be called the "bride of Christ." David allowed the mysteries and revelations to do what they were intended to do—impact his heart. That is why the Holy Spirit revealed the mystery. Even that idea is a revelation we need to let sink in.

Paul knew that when you receive clarity, you will have longevity in your pursuit. His prayer for the church of Ephesus, found in Ephesians 1, was: *The way to keep the church in Ephesus strong, mature, and moving on in the things of God is through revealing mysteries in the knowledge of Him. Eyes of their heart, touch them! Take off the blinders and the haze! Father, put eye salve on them and allow them to begin to see clearly with the eyes of their heart.* The Holy Spirit reveals these mysteries to keep us fascinated for eternity. The mysteries of this Man are endless because they are so deep. We can be fascinated for eternity.

Unfortunately, the reality is that it's easier to worry about life than be fascinated. I worry about business. I worry about "Dwayne Roberts' International Ministry." I worry about my impact, my calling, the program results, the things I am supposed to do and how I am supposed to do them; the loan, the degree, the finances. Life issues—business, finances, demands, expectations, goals—begin to get in my way and stop me from seeing clearly.

But the beautiful thing is that the ones who understand the importance of revelation will know that it is the true gift they need to cherish. And they will once again refocus their life to put the first things first.

The other day I saw a fast-food contest that guaranteed a prize every time you played (like free fries or a drink). A big retailer offered a chance for a car and a $3,000 shopping spree in exchange for your email address. What is it about us that believes we should get something just for blinking or breathing? We want to be rewarded for doing things we would do anyway. Saving up isn't good enough—we want exponential interest growth as well. Granted ... here's a 401(k), an IRA, and an annuity. One penny in the wishing well, ten pennies back, right? Not only do we want to get the prize, we want it to be worth many times more than what we put in ... here's the state lottery and a few slot machines. Be honest. Wouldn't you be totally floored if $100,000 went into your bank account just for, oh I don't know, buying this book? Who would turn that down?

There are mysteries sitting in front of you today that would bring more reward than $100,000. Even if you won a million dollars without being taxed, it would only sustain you for thirty years or so. But your soul will exist for eternity—what will sustain it?

We have said that loving God is the first and foremost thing in life, the ultimate priority, and one of only a few things that will exist far beyond eternity. Love never fails or stops. It is without end because love began in God and He has no end. You desire to love Him. You want to experience Him. If you can let yourself receive His love and understand that He delights in you, you have won an enormous battle. The divine gold mine is waiting to be discovered. Your journey will be very personal, but since it takes God to love God, you will undoubtedly feel the Lord touch your heart with His affection so that you are equipped to love Him back.

God has issued an invitation to you—open the Scriptures and look upon this Man, Jesus Christ. At the end of the day, it does not matter what is in the bank. Too many times, we get so caught up in our overwhelming daily tasks and problems that we fail to realize and acknowledge the simplicity of the First Commandment, the passion worth pursuing—giving your love and your life to Jesus. The important questions to ask are: What do I understand of the knowledge of God, and what is settled within my inner man concerning Him? Does Jesus fascinate my heart and am I energized by His delight in me? Is there anything else on earth worth pursuing?

LIKED
BY
GOD

06

ISAIAH'S MESSAGE

For so long we have heard that "God is love" (1 John 4:16). But if we don't connect to the reality of that verse, it easily loses its impact. One of the defining moments in my life was when I realized that God not only loved me, but also liked me. While that may sound somewhat childish or elementary, it is now deep within the foundation of my life. I am liked by God!

After living in Kansas City for about a year, I heard a message from Isaiah 62 that completely changed the course of my life. That may sound like a pretty grandiose statement, but it was really all about my spiritual life, which is the key to my existence. Once my "life in God" began to improve, the other components of my life fell into place as well (although it wasn't automatic like dutiful robots). The converse is also true: if your spiritual life is in the gutter, so goes the rest of life. Sadly, some people just get used to that.

Isaiah was a prophet during Hezekiah's reign, around 700 B.C. There was a certain amount of prosperity in the land, yet Isaiah was prophesying of a time to come when the nation would be in turmoil, when the Babylonian empire would invade their nation and take them captive. As an inhabitant, Isaiah spoke from his own perspective a lot. But as a prophet, he often spoke from God's point of view as well. In this chapter, Isaiah's heart melded with the Lord's in this emotional exclamation, and he found himself prophesying to the nation from the perspective of God's heart, speaking of the coming crisis and what it would mean for them.

> "For Zion's sake I will not hold My peace, and for Jerusalem's sake I will not rest, until her righteousness goes forth as brightness, and her salvation as a lamp that burns." —Isaiah 62:1, NKJV

The Lord was making a commitment to them, saying that in the middle of this national takeover, He was utterly committed to their well-being—but He wanted their hearts. It's the same thing the God of desire had been saying for eons. He called them repeatedly because He was intent on having a people who loved Him, yet they did not listen to His call. They rejected the prophets, silenced their own inner witness, and wandered. But He continued to be consumed with righteous desire (jealousy) for their hearts. His tone is unmistakable in the words of desire and unrelenting that He chose: *I will not hold My peace, and I will not rest until you are bright and burning!* He had done the whisper for decades, and now He was bringing in discipline and a certain amount of chastening for them to fully run to Him. It would be rough on them for quite a while because—and this is key—He wanted their hearts completely. They were about to find themselves in a certain amount of despair as a nation. But He gave them the one message ahead of time that would sustain them: *I am committed to making you a fiery people, and I will not rest until it is done, even though it may appear unjust to the human mind.*

I believe this word was specifically for Jerusalem, but I also believe it is for us today as well. God is committed to me. I will go into dark places, and the light I carry will penetrate the darkness. God is committed to you; wherever you go, He will rest upon you and create profound breakthrough. He is committed to that. The word of the Lord to Isaiah was, "The Gentiles shall see your righteousness, and all kings your glory" (Isa. 62:2, NKJV). He was saying that the lost were going to recognize His Church one day. Your bosses, the team captains on the sports field, the heads of state, and rulers of nations will recognize His people. From the lowest worker to the highest CEO, it will be obvious to them. The unrelenting energy, the heart consumed with desire, and the perfect will of the Creator are fixed on making His people a bright and shining blaze, a lamp set on a hill.

Isaiah continued by giving them insight into their eternal identity, even though it unleashed a certain amount of national despair. He let them know what was coming around the bend … life in a foreign land, under an oppressive rule; a feeling of being completely forsaken; the experience of utter despair without hope and a deep heart-disruption that would touch their very core. As a people, they would be overtaken internally and externally. But the Lord had an ace up His sleeve, a sure-fire winner. He was going to tell them who they were, calming the despair within and giving them something they had not felt for quite some time: an unchanging identity springing from the eternal God.

> *"You shall be called by a new name, which the mouth of the Lord will name." —Isaiah 62:2, NKJV*

Basically, this means the Holy Spirit was going to reveal the Father's heart toward them. And—surprise—it wasn't bad! In fact, it was royalty; He felt royalty toward them. His major strategy to conquer their despair was to tell them how He felt about them. They were the highest of the high, the greatest of the great—royalty in the hand of God Himself.

> *"You shall also be a crown of glory in the hand of the Lord, and a royal diadem in the hand of your God." —Isaiah 62:3, NKJV*

We interrupt this history lesson for a reality check: I was feeling a certain amount of failure in my life. What did being invaded by an enemy nation have to do with that?

Remember "Dwayne Roberts' International Ministry"? It was going to be huge. Global, even. But I wanted to quit. I saw those things my mother once spoke over me slipping quickly away. The reality was that I was sitting there bewildered, thinking, *Have I completely missed it and failed? I can hardly pay our bills; I've got one young child; the pressures of life are building; and I can't even tell you the last time my heart felt moved. Have I failed?* I felt considerably disillusioned.

Today, as I look into the heart of the Church, I see disillusionment filling the body of Christ; there is bewilderment with the Creator and with the religious systems. As I said before, I think the average believer sits in the pew, internally screaming, *Where are You? I don't feel You, I don't know You, and I have no idea what You even think about me.* All the while he feels despair and disillusionment invading his heart, and he truly believes he is defenseless. Sadly, I think this is how much of the Church lives today; their willingness to admit it is another issue.

And that's where I found myself. I didn't know how to articulate what was going on, but I was not happy in my inner man. My heart was hardened. Now that I can be honest, I will admit that I felt a great boredom with God. When I prayed, it would usually be about circumstances in my life: *Give me wisdom in this; let me have blessing in that; we need a breakthrough here,* and on and on. Or I would go into my room, open my Bible, close my eyes, and sit ... and nothing would happen. I didn't know what to say. I didn't know what to do.

In truth, there was a calloused hardness in my heart, though I was supposedly a minister of the Gospel, a proclaimer. The truth is, I was going hard after ministry because I believed that ministering was the mandate over my life. Well, it wasn't. Never has been, never will be. Ministering and serving are not the goal, and they aren't the issue here. We know because in this Isaiah passage, the Lord didn't spend much time commenting on their career path. Rather, He hit deeper issues ... heart stuff. That's what He was after—their hearts.

THE DELIGHT OF GOD

Let me clarify something because I don't want to turn you off if you don't necessarily feel called to ministry. There's no difference between me and someone else who happens to be an educator, businessperson, carpenter, athlete, musician, or artist. God has placed an amazing individual destiny before each of us, and there is no shame in wanting to see it through to its glorious end. With that said, though, making that your end goal will leave you disillusioned and bewildered. And, you see, that was my end goal.

Sure, I was sort of naïve and ignorant. For all I knew, this was who I was, and I had the drive, so there was no reason not to do it. However, my identity was wrapped up in it. If I did great, I felt great; if I didn't do so great, I felt defeated. But if you ever tried to separate me from ministry, I would have thought you'd ripped out my soul, my very core, and just left it writhing as you waited for it to stop gasping.

But for some odd reason, as I listened to the sermon that day, the speaker said, "I'm going to speak a new name over you," and my insides stopped convulsing. All of a sudden I was listening and paying attention. I was waiting to hear the next few phrases because … well, I didn't really know why. I just knew that I had grasped something deep and soul-encompassing within me. God was speaking to my heart, and what He was saying had the power to change the most incredible zealot or depressed legalist into the most passionate, joyous person.

> *"You shall no longer be termed Forsaken, nor*
> *shall your land any more be termed Desolate;*
> *but you shall be called Hephzibah, and your*
> *land Beulah; for the Lord delights in you, and*

your land shall be married." —Isaiah 62:4,
NKJV

I had been feeling a little disillusioned, a little bit lost, and a little bit broken. I wasn't suicidal or anything like that, but I was struggling in a major way. But as these words were spoken, I could actually feel them. The Holy Spirit revealed them in a specific way, and I felt the delight of God weighing on my heart. He was making good on His ancient promise to reveal His heart toward me. All the things we feel—abandoned, deserted, alone, isolated, depressed, bewildered—will no longer define who we are. The Holy Spirit gives us our identity.

And what is the identity He has chosen for us? What is the principal thing God thinks and feels when you come to mind? He delights in you. Another way of putting it is to say, "God, You like me." Now after not meeting my goals, struggling with the life equation, quitting the ministry, and falling a bit short, the Holy Spirit began to open my eyes to the heart of God. All of a sudden, I started to catch a bit of what God, the Creator, thinks about me whenever He looks at me. In my heart, I was ecstatic but cautious. *What? I've never heard this before! I would love it if it were true, but ... could it be?*

So I began to say, "Tell me again. I'm a twenty-nine-year-old man, and I need to know what my God thinks about me." More and more it was dawning on me that God has emotions. And He has some pretty overwhelming ones when it comes to me. He started to look less like the flannelgraph Deity from Sunday school or the disinterested, mad, and overbearing rule-enforcer I was always hiding from. I put that verse into my prayer using my own language: *You like me. God, You like me. When You look at me, Your heart begins to move toward me. When my name is spoken in heaven, a smile crosses Your face.* This may sound overly simplistic, but when you pray using Scripture as a guide, it starts to change little things inside your heart (which turn out to be big things by the time it's all said and done). I was starting to believe that God, the Creator, just might enjoy me. And it made me want to really find out what was in His heart toward me.

> *"For as a young man marries a virgin, so shall your sons marry you; and as the bridegroom rejoices over the bride, so shall your God rejoice over you." —Isaiah 62:5, NKJV*

The last part of this verse is astounding. Consider this: In our own lives we have seen people in love ... you've maybe even experienced that feeling yourself. It's elation beyond belief. You could soar without even trying. You could walk on water, float on air, even clean your room if there was a hint that person was coming over. You start missing appointments, leaving work early, and ditching lifelong friends just to have a few more moments with the one who moves your heart so effortlessly. The way you spend your time, energy, and money changes ... it is now focused on some rapturous being who has consumed your attention. That same feeling, that very same heart-pounding, voracious desire, is what moves the heavenly Bridegroom, Jesus.

Somehow in the service that morning I began to understand that the God of creation has the same passion for me bursting from His heart. Just as a bridegroom looks at a bride with joy and desire, the Creator has that same motivation toward me. Gradually, I was being touched and awakened by these revelations.

God delights in human beings. More specifically, God really does delight in you; He sings, dances, and is filled with joy at the thought of you. Right now this may sound a bit too much like fantasy; most of us have simply been told to love God without any kind of instruction on how that can be done—or, more to the point, *why* it can be done (we'll get into the practicals in chapter 8). We've all heard the normal answer: "Pray, read the Bible, and go to church." While the old standbys are certainly more profound than we give them credit for, these responses far from answer your real questions or energize your heart to see it through. Sure, you can grit your teeth and push through the pain, but humans can do things through willpower alone for only a short time. Then reality sets in, and the normalcy of everyday life erodes that will power, leaving you asking, *Why should I continue on like this?* It seems futile and pointless.

But passion changes everything, and that was exactly what the Lord was getting at in Isaiah. Passion is the key ingredient that changes duty to desire, "have to and ought to" to "love to and can't wait to." Would you rather marry for passion or to demonstrate your maturity and discipline? And what would a grand epic battle be worth if it were simply an exercise in duty? No one wants to watch a movie where the battle is fought out of duty, but it's compelling when there is an irresistible belief in the premise of the war. Ask any man if he would rather discover that his wife is being intimate with him out of marital duty or desire. The answer is the same every time: he wants her heart. This is only natural; no young kid dreams of someday fulfilling his obligations. Kids want to live their dreams, their passion. They are moved on the inside, and they want to pursue their dreams. Faithfulness and patient endurance certainly are hallmarks of faith, but passion … oh, there is simply no substitute. In fact, no amount of perseverance can make up for spine-tingling ardor—

but on the other hand, that same ardor will make you persevere through anything!

Look at David and his heart again. He pursued God in a focused way. He answered the call to one thing. He touched the delight of God, and it ruined him for anything less. Psalm 16:3 shows how well David understood the Lord's heart for His people. "As for the saints who are on the earth, 'they are the excellent ones, in whom is all my delight'" (NKJV). David's passion existed because he actually felt the delight of God upon his own heart. He was able to love because he felt love. He was able to delight himself in God because he felt God's delight in him.

When we feel the Lord's passion for us, when we really know that He likes us, when we feel His constant smile upon our hearts, we will be ignited with passion for Him as well. There's no substitute for feeling the love bubbling up from His heart toward you. He really likes you. Love is the main motivation of His heart, all day, every day, without fail and without hesitation. That's why "God is love." It's constant and overflowing, and it is forever aimed at you—with the goal of winning your heart completely. As much as a bridegroom desires his bride, God desires you—precisely because He is a Bridegroom and you are His bride.

DEFINED BY GOD'S AFFECTION

I have three incredible kids: Sydney, Chloe, and Elijah. As a father, when I look at my three children, it's hard to quantify or describe how much each has found a place in my heart. It's not a math equation. I'm just so in love with them. We recently took a vacation, and it furthered our bond. They grew deeper into my heart even through the expected "family tensions." They would fights among themselves, get mad at Jennifer and me, and begin to get into trouble—but all it did was draw me closer to them. I could see that their straying would get them into harm in another ten steps, and that endeared them to me in a greater way, so I began to pursue them.

Let's say in a few years we find that one of my kids does something really stupid at age sixteen. Certainly I would feel a twinge of disappointment, but it would be more of a hurting for them than outright rage at them. I will want to pursue them with greater passion and more tangible actions because the pain of seeing them hurt themselves will be stronger than the feelings of frustration toward the situation.

As I began to think about this, it hit me: we are defined by how God feels about us, and God's delight is not defined by our failures or successes. As we grow in the revelation of His delight and His pursuit of us, it begins to define who we are as individuals. So in the midst of feeling disillusioned and a bit like a failure, I began to feel His delight spoken over me in this sermon on Isaiah. All of a sudden, it awakened me to the reality that my failures and my successes have never changed His view of me, His delight in me, or His pursuit of me. And, all of a sudden, I felt the Creator lean down toward me in greater measure. He was pursuing me by opening my eyes and giving me revelation. He was going after me by allowing me to see Him; He was giving Himself to me. My heart began to soften toward Him. Then I actually began to feel His affection. I sat there, feeling this love penetrate my heart, and it awakened love for Jesus within me. In the same way a bridegroom takes joy in his bride, He was rejoicing in me.

Each one of us is defined by what God thinks about us. His thoughts and feelings are your true identity, whether you understand it or not. The problem is that we are generally so separated from this whole other realm that we don't notice what is going on in the Lord's heart moment by moment. It leaves us with only one option: to just believe things that are not true about His nature. *I messed up way too badly this time, so I guess I have to repent harder, pray longer, and do more good things today than I normally do so He'll restore me ... I need to find a way to make it up to Him ... He's bound to be angrier with me this time than last time.*

When you understand that He delights in you, it will change how you relate to Him. We are defined by what God says about us, but too often we have bought into lies about Him and His nature. What if you really did believe that He fully enjoys you as you are? Wouldn't it make you want to be with Him more? Wouldn't it actually engender a certain amount of desire toward Him? And wouldn't all those commandments take on a different tone? You might even find yourself wanting to do what He asks. Suddenly your entire relationship would feel different; it may even look different to someone on the outside. It would look like you want to do it, you enjoy doing it, you desire to do it, instead of like you are merely supposed to do it.

THE FIRST COMMANDMENT: PASSION AND ENJOYMENT

Have you ever actually pondered the First Commandment? It's unbelievable. It requires so much. God said, *I want you to have love.* What He meant was, *I want you to be tender. When the name of Jesus is spoken, I want it to move you toward Him. When His name is spoken, I want you to weep.* But, of course, He didn't stop there. He said, *I want all your money to line up with your heart toward Me. I want all of your time to line up with your desire for Me. I want all of your strength, all of your energy, all of your pursuits to fall in line with your tenderness toward Me.*

I've always looked at passionate people and thought, *I want to be passionate about something.* I want to have passion about rock climbing, bicycling, golfing, stamp collecting, running, anything. Then I see people with passion for Jesus. They are a rare but growing breed, especially in this generation, but hopefully you have seen one or two. It is appealing to see people who actually want to give up things just to make more room in their lives to love Jesus. They clear the clutter and devote that portion of their time and energy to pursuing Him more earnestly. Inch by inch they take back their inner life in God, the things hidden to the outside world, and turn them over to the God they have found to be Love. The crazy thing is that this revelation of Jesus and His heart for me, this love the Bridegroom has for His bride, began to hit me in a pretty deep way. I was twenty-nine, and I found myself awakened to really loving Jesus. I began to rearrange my life because I wanted to pursue Him. Not to pursue ministry, but to pursue Jesus.

Granted, I've been raised in the church. My brother prayed me into the kingdom when I was six years old because he was worried I had a first-class ticket to hell. Early on I bought into the lie that my mandate was to pursue my ministry, and so, naturally, that's what I did. Until only a few years ago, I had spent my entire existence with the aim of getting "Dwayne Roberts' International Ministry" off the ground and making mine a household name. But just maybe there was hope for me … the reality was finally sinking in that my pursuit in life should really be about Jesus. If you do the math, you'll see that I've been saved for about twenty-five years, and it is only now that I'm finding out about what I'm really supposed to run after.

It's called the First Commandment. It's called "Jesus, I love You with everything I've got, and I want to pursue You all the days of my life." This is what I'm about. This is where I want to go. Whenever His name is spoken, I want it to compel me to run harder after this Man.

As I was sitting, listening to the sermon on the Isaiah passage, my prayer was, *Oh, please tell me more because I want to know all that is in Your heart toward me. Jesus, please speak to me. Holy Spirit, bring revelation of the knowledge of Your love toward me. I have to know it.* The Holy Spirit was taking the mysteries of 1 Corinthians 2 and making them real to me, freely giving them to me. I didn't somehow bribe Him to do it; He just did it as I set my heart toward God. It was a free gift, and it was overwhelming my heart.

This unbelievable, immeasurable gift is waiting in front of you. The Holy Spirit is searching out revelations, going deeper and deeper and deeper into the character and the heart of the Creator. Then He turns around and freely offers it to anyone who has his heart set toward the Son of Man. So you as a believer—weak, broken, disillusioned, immature—with this little "yes" in your heart can stand up in the midst of friends and enemies and say, "I am setting my heart to love the Son of God." The Holy Spirit is waiting, watching, ready to pursue anyone who says "yes." And when you do, an incredible spiritual feast is set out before you: the Holy Spirit begins to offer you revelation in the knowledge of this One called God.

That is what was happening to me, and it is on the Lord's heart to do this with all of us. He wants to tell us our new name in such a profound way that it changes the very foundation of our heart—our eternal identity. The Holy Spirit fully intends to reveal what is in the heart of God toward you. How will He do it? He will reveal the eternal mysteries—the love and desire of God for you—to your heart.

He simply started to speak to my heart. "Dwayne, you have no idea what I think about you. You feel like you've failed, like your future is gone, and you're going to be a garbage man the rest of your life. But My heart is bursting with emotion for you. From the first moment I set My eyes upon you in your mother's womb, My affections and desires have never changed. I've always looked upon you with joy, delight, and passion. I have great plans for you." The Holy Spirit was revealing the heart of God to me. It wooed me and awakened me.

THE KNOWLEDGE OF GOD

At IHOP-KC, we pray Ephesians 1:17-19 over the city all the time because Isaiah and Paul told us it is the desire of God's heart: *Holy Spirit, reveal the Son of Man to us. Give us wisdom and revelation in the knowledge of God. We are asking that the things You've learned about the God of creation, about the Son of Man with burning desire and passion, You would make known to us as weak and immature believers. We need to know what the Creator thinks about us this morning. Jesus, tell us afresh. We must know what is in Your heart toward us today. We have to touch it. We have to feel it.*

The knowledge of God is an overwhelming concept. But the Holy Spirit, with incredible vigor, is searching out this knowledge and freely giving it to anyone who says, "I want to love Jesus, I want to feel Jesus, I want to know Jesus." The Holy Spirit is beginning to lay out an enormous, divine banquet for us.

I want to call your attention to the first chapter of Ephesians.

If you visit IHOP-KC, you'll hear it prayed about twenty times a day. It's a cry from the heart of Paul: *Church in Ephesus, you must know the Son of Man, because it is going to be the stabilizing factor and the foundational value of your existence. It will make you strong and mature.*

I have found that I am becoming more confident and less worried about what people think about me. Negative thoughts about me do not have the same impact they used to. The bottom line is, whether I'm standing on a stage or cleaning the toilet, God likes me. I want this to be the defining message over my life—God likes me. That is the foundation of my identity. Whether it's a good day or a bad day, I am not on an emotional roller coaster because my heart finds stability in the fact that I am loved by the Creator. I am defined by the constant reality of God's affection for me.

Revelation 12:10 tells us that the devil is standing before the throne of God, accusing you night and day. He's lying to you on a daily basis about the nature and the heart of God. He's constantly telling you lies that you've bought into and believed, and that you now act out of. My prayer is that the lies of the accuser would be broken and their influence would become void in your life. I pray that you would be defined by the Creator who made you from His delight and desire and that you would become who He actually intended you to be.

At the end of the day, we are defined by how God feels about us, and God's delight is not defined by our failures or successes. He has created you to spend eternity with His Son, not to pursue ministry opportunities or temporal success. That is what you were made for—it is your destiny, your eternal future. It's what I referred to earlier as the "Bridal Paradigm"; you are meant to rule and reign in a bridal, intimate relationship with the Son of Man for eternity. And to that end, it is imperative that you know what is in His heart: not anger or frustration, but utter desire—heart-pounding, voracious desire that moves Jesus to pursue you day after day. He likes you, and He longs for your affection. He is after your heart. So shall your God rejoice over you.

When I finally realized that God liked me, it changed the way I related to Him and others on a daily basis. God was committed to giving that revelation to my heart, and He is committed to touching you with the same understanding. The Holy Spirit fully intends to reveal what is in the heart of God toward you because there is simply no substitute for feeling the love that bubbles up inside His heart. It will awaken love for Jesus within you as it did in me.

Jesus rejoices over you. The Lord delights in you. This is not disappointment and frustration, but pure delight and enjoyment. God likes you so much that He came after you. While sin still separated you from Him, He set His affection upon you and pursued you. I pray this would be a revelation that would stir and awaken you. May the power of God's affections pierce your heart and awaken you to ever-increasing love for this Man.

PIERCED
BY
THE
DIVINE

I WOULD DIE FOR YOU

Imagine being one of Jesus' twelve closest friends during His final hours, looking into His eyes, sitting, eating, and having conversation—unaware that you are only hours away from seeing Him beaten, ridiculed, and nailed upon a cross. The last portion of the book of John is phenomenal, and I cannot help but imagine myself as one of His disciples in this setting.

Jesus was having a conversation with his friends, knowing fully what was about to happen to Him and all of creation. He knew the game plan. He knew the blows of the upcoming battle. He knew the pain ahead. Yet He was clear and focused on the glorious victory at the end of it all. Jesus—fully God, fully Man—sat with humanity, conversing in affection with the very ones for whom He would soon be crucified.

In John 13, Jesus looked at these friends and told them He was about to leave. We need to understand their belief that He would stay around to be crowned king. They actually thought Jesus was going to be the political leader of their day, through some sort of righteous anarchy. Suddenly He told them He was about to leave them, and not just leave—He was about to be betrayed by a friend, left by those around the table, mutilated by those in power, and sacrificed in the cruelest known way. This was a blow out of nowhere, the shock of a lifetime, and they were confused: *What are You talking about? Aren't You coming to set up Your throne and Your kingdom?*

Then in verses 36-38, Peter made a bold statement. "Simon Peter said to Him, 'Lord, where are You going?' Jesus answered him, 'Where I am going you cannot follow Me now, but you shall follow Me afterward.' Peter said to Him, 'Lord, why can I not follow You now? I will lay down my life for Your sake.' Jesus answered him, 'Will you lay down your life for My sake? Most assuredly, I say to you, the rooster shall not crow till you have denied Me three times'" (NKJV).

Peter is known for his boldness, but make no mistake: he meant what he said. Peter trusted this Man; he believed in Him, followed Him, and truly loved Him. Peter meant what he said to Jesus in those last hours. He did not care where Jesus was going or what He was about to do—he was committed to Christ in every way. Jesus had brought incredible transformation to him. When Peter looked into the eyes of Jesus, he could feel the Lord piercing through to the innermost part of his being. Peter had made up his mind quite a while ago; even if the others flaked out, he was still going to be committed to following Him all the days of his life, even to the point of laying down his life for Him. Peter would die for Him.

IMMATURE SINCERITY

Have you ever made a similar statement? Maybe not specifically concerning death, but perhaps other spiritual vows? *For the next month I will be up at 5:00 a.m. to read the Word ... I am going to talk about Jesus to someone on my campus every day this week— I'm going for it ... I will never commit that sin again.* Many times we unknowingly find ourselves saying the same things as Peter: "I will follow You all the days of my life; I'll never deny You; I'll die for You." As we know from the story, only hours later Peter was tested on his words: *Hey, weren't you with that Jesus guy?* As soon as the heat came, three times Peter shouted, *I don't know the Man! I am not associated with Him!* I imagine all of a sudden Jesus' eyes focused in on Peter as the rooster crowed. Peter was cut to the heart.

This is the very same man who boasted that he would follow Christ. He had a massive "yes" in his heart. Jesus had touched him and changed his life. Yet his flesh was weak, and he was unable to live out the sincerity that was in his heart. The Bible tells us that Peter "wept bitterly." He wept because he could not follow through on his devotion. He was torn because he could not follow through on the commitment he made. His spirit was willing, but his flesh was weak.

I love this because of how Peter's story ends. The very guy who completely failed Jesus in His greatest hour of suffering was the first one to preach about the resurrection. That is amazing!

In those final hours, Jesus was in need of support from His buddies, but He stood alone. Peter, who looked up at Him and said, "I will follow You all the days of my life," completely failed Him. Not only did Peter simply not do what he said he would, the pendulum completely swung the other way; he went so far as to deny ever meeting Jesus.

Talk about a nose dive. Peter was a ball of flaming cement! Talk about weakness, failure, and disappointment; talk about a seemingly hopeless case. But wait … weeks later, Peter—dust shaken off his body, power resting on him—boldly proclaimed, "He is risen!" Thousands responded, and it turned out that the betrayer was the very one preaching the Gospel, fulfilling the calling upon his life.

BACK ON YOUR FEET

What was it about Peter that, when he realized it was the Son of Man who had died and now was alive, made him abandon everything? He found out it was Jesus on the waves, and he immediately dove in and couldn't wait to embrace Him. What did Peter know about Jesus that allowed him to do that with confidence? If that were me—if I had blown it that bad—I would be at the back of the line, feeling about an inch tall, kicking my feet in the dirt, thinking, "I wonder what He thinks about me, this Man who so touched my life. I wonder what He is thinking about me now that I've denied Him."

Not Peter. He couldn't wait to get close to Jesus and be embraced. Peter knew something that caused him to rise from complete failure. There was something experiential in his foundation that helped him overcome shame. This weak betrayer knew something about this Man, and it gave him complete boldness and desire to immediately run into His arms and embrace Him.

Jesus had so impacted Peter that after Peter completely failed, he could rise in confidence weeks later and preach the Gospel. He was growing in his faith, being discipled under the very Son of God, but he was still immature. He had a big "yes" on the inside, but his flesh was not able to maintain what was in his heart. Peter was weak in the same ways we are, yet he arose with an undeniable confidence.

ABIDE IN THE VINE

I think part of what Peter felt, what gave him boldness, actually came from the last words Jesus spoke to him in the book of John. Before Jesus made His final speech to the disciples (found in John 14-16), He had already prophesied to Peter about what he would do that night. The rooster's crow did not come as a surprise to Jesus.

Jesus could have gone to the religious institutions of the hour. He could have walked up and chosen any of the prestigious religious leaders of that day and said, *I am going to give you My kingdom. I am about to leave, and you are the ones I have chosen to take My kingdom.* That would seem like the most logical conclusion. Instead, He gathered together His twelve disciples, inexperienced twentysomethings, and said to them, *Guys, I'm leaving, but I'm looking to you as the ones who are going to build My Church. I have confidence in you to lead My kingdom. My rule is going to rest on the shoulders of twentysomethings … immature, with great propensity to weakness, stumbling often. I choose you.*

But Jesus did not leave them unequipped. He gave them something to ensure that they would have strength and confidence to build the kingdom.

"I am the true vine, and My Father is the vinedresser. Every branch in Me that does not bear fruit He takes away; and every branch that bears fruit He prunes, that it may bear more fruit. You are already clean because of the word which I have spoken to you. Abide in Me, and I in you. As the branch cannot bear fruit of itself, unless it abides in the vine, neither can you, unless you abide in Me."
—John 15:1-4, NKJV

Jesus looked into their eyes and said, *Here's the key. This is the truth you need to remember and focus on: you and I abiding in each other. I'm talking about you and Me having life flowing back and forth, revelation and life pouring into your spirit, My words resonating within you, closing your eyes and having Me speak to your heart. If you do that, if you and I abide in life together, you will have fruit. I am the vine, you are the branches. He who abides in Me, and I in him, bears much fruit. For without Me, you can do nothing.*

If you feel a call to ministry, if you think you want to be a preacher, pastor, or teacher, read this verse, highlight it, write it on your mirror: *Without Me you can do nothing.* When you wake up in the morning, you'll see it.

I am going to say something heavy now. My fear—a true fear I have—is that the leadership in the Western Church has totally stepped out of this reality and has chosen to build the kingdom of God on a program-based reality, which most of us have joined in on. Sadly, we are content to live without receiving divine life.

I bought into this once, and I still struggle with it in some ways because that default mechanism is ingrained within me. But I have now bought into the reality that I have life in my inner being, that the resurrected Son of Man and I are abiding together, and that something of substance is being spoken into my spirit. I have a big goal in mind. I want to live from a place of receiving and interacting with the divine because Jesus said if I do that, I will have life and fruitfulness. But if I don't walk in a life of prayer, in a life of intimacy, I cannot do anything.

DID JESUS REALLY SAY THAT?

The first eight verses of John 15 speak powerfully about the reality of a life in ministry. I love them. However, verse 9 is the real kicker. Jesus had just told them they were all going to deny Him. Young Pete jumped up and said, *Not me! They may flake out, but I will follow You to my death!* Then, as Jesus went on, He said, *Peter, I want to make sure I have your attention. Look in my eyes right now.* Then He said to all the disciples, *As the eternal Father has loved Me—as the Father has looked down upon Me, and I have felt His affections resting upon Me, as My heart has been expanded because of His devotion, His desire, and His longing, as we interact with overwhelming love for one another—as the Father has loved Me, so I now love you, just as you are.*

The very devotion, desire, and longing that the Father has for the Son is the same that Jesus has focused on you. This is mind-blowing. There is no deeper relationship, in my opinion, than that of the Eternal Father and the Eternal Son. The Father is looking upon His Son Jesus, and He feels intense delight and desire. He looks upon Him and says, *Jesus, My Son, I long for You! You are My Son, and I desire You.*

The resurrected Son, Jesus, with His heart full and alive, then turned and looked at the young man by His side. *Peter, I know what you are going to do tonight. Your weakness is not a surprise to Me at all. In fact, the first day that I looked upon you and called you, I knew your temperament; I knew your strengths and was fully aware of your weaknesses. Nothing is a surprise to Me. Even knowing your weakness and your propensity to sin, desire for you bursts forth from My heart. Peter, I chose you in the midst of your weakness, not in your greatest hour of strength when you felt like you had something to offer. Peter, as the Father has loved Me, so I now set My affection upon you. I want You to abide in My love.*

You know what that means? When you get up in the morning, Jesus wants you to feel His desire upon you. He doesn't want merely an intellectual interaction. He wants the desire and emotion that flow from His heart to touch your heart, and then be poured back from you upon Him. He truly is a Bridegroom in love. He desires that you abide in Him as He abides in you. Jesus is just looking for any time when He can get your gaze. It has nothing to do with your performance and productivity. He chose you, and He is still choosing you. He has always known your future—your successes and your failures. In the context of all of that, He sets His desire and His longing upon you, and He pursues you—even unto death—because He wants you, because He made you for Himself.

This is not some casual, "You're a decent chap … and besides, it looks like you're having a good hair day." No! This is the eternal God saying, "I long for you! I have desires that I want to tell you about. I want you to know that when your name is spoken in My courts, longing bursts forth in My heart!"

Think about it ... God desires us. It is passion that sent Him to the cross, not dry obligation or necessity. Nothing was going to hold Him back. Nothing was going to get in His way. He does not have a running pro and con list about you so He can quantify the amount of love you deserve—Jesus simply and fully desires you!

OUR GOD NAMED DESIRE

Because our God is filled with emotions, He does not take an intellectual approach to the human heart. It's not, "God is mental comprehension, or knowledge, or brains." No, 1 John 4 says our God is love. You know what that means? God is desire. God is passion. God is fervor and ardor and zeal. He is filled with emotion. God has longing for us because that is who He is. He cannot be anything different than that. His character is unchanging. He calls Himself Love. He calls Himself Desire.

Yet have you noticed how we automatically question His affection and His nature whenever we fail? We immediately think He is out to pay us back or that we must do something to regain His favor. Do we actually think that our best day of perfection is worthy of the affections of the King of the Universe? *You were perfect today, My child. Well done. I can now say that I have enjoyed you all day ... we'll just have to see how you do tomorrow, but I doubt you can keep it up.* Our best and worst days are equal under the love of this Man. We can do nothing to earn His pursuit.

There was something about Jesus that convinced Peter of this. When Peter was out weeping bitterly, after he had completely blown it, I believe he thought back to his conversation with Jesus only a few hours earlier. He remembered Jesus looking in his eyes and the way it made his heart feel. Then he realized something: *Oh, my gosh—Jesus—He knew what I was going to do; He prophesied it. He was fully aware. And even though He knew I would deny Him, He still said to me, "My Father loves Me, Peter, so I love you."* Then, in the midst of his shame and brokenness, Peter began to rise.

Peter was becoming rooted and grounded in the love of Ephesians 3, the love that knows no height, no length, no depth, no breadth, no end whatsoever; he was being rooted and grounded in understanding the heart of Jesus. As a twentysomething, he was realizing, *I am loved by the King! He desires me! He formed me. He knew what I was going to do, and even in that place, He loved me!* The Holy Spirit gave Peter revelation of this One he walked with and was devoted to. He remembered Jesus' words and the look in His eyes, and boldness and confidence arose within him. Encountering Jesus brought revelation, and revelation brought confidence in His love.

This young adult discovered that Jesus liked him, and he arose with authority on his life. The foundation of his life was more than, "Well, maybe if I catch Him at a good moment, He won't smite me." The deepest belief in his heart was the familiar Sunday school chorus, "Jesus loves me, this I know." Peter knew in the depths of his being that the desire of Jesus was for him, even as a betrayer. I believe Peter tested the boundaries, but every time he messed up, he asked the same questions we all have in our hearts: Is it true? Is there longing in His heart for me that never subsides? Have I messed up too badly this time? Does He still love me, will He forgive me, and will He take me back?

THE FATHER'S AFFECTION

"And the glory which You gave Me I have given

them, that they may be one just as We are one:
I in them, and You in Me; that they may be
made perfect in one, and that the world may
know that You have sent Me, and have loved
them as You have loved Me." —John 17:22-23,
NKJV

Take a look at that last phrase again: "You have loved them as You have loved Me." Jesus prayed to the eternal Father, *Father, I want unity within My Church. I want them to be one. And I want them to know that You love them as much as You love Me.*

He was praying for His disciples. And He was praying for us—you and me. He cried out, *Father in Heaven, I want them to know one thing: the desire in Your heart for Me is exactly the same as the desire that You have for them.* If it weren't written in the Word of God, from the lips of Jesus, I don't think I would believe it.

One time, while meditating on this verse, I pictured it this way: I was standing beside God's only Son, shoulder to shoulder. The Creator, the eternal Father, was looking down upon both of us. He first fixed His gaze on Jesus. He said, "Jesus, Jesus, My Son, I love You. Every time I look at You, longing is in My heart toward You. You have won My heart—oh, it just overflows when I look upon You. I long for You, Jesus." He then fixed His gaze on me and, gathering the same intensity and emotion as when He spoke to Jesus, He said my name. "Dwayne, My son, I knit you with such care in your mother's womb. Dwayne, when I, the Creator and eternal Father, look upon you, I am so proud of you. The enemy desires to steal, to kill, and to destroy your life. But I sit in the courts of heaven with such longing and such desire bursting forth from My heart toward you. Oh, you have no idea how My heart overflows when I look upon you! You are My beloved son, the delight of My heart!"

I was overwhelmed. I prayed, "Let this pierce me, God. I want to know what is in Your heart toward me. Father, convince me, overwhelm me with the desire that is in Your heart." God the Father knew everything about me, and even before I could turn toward Him, He said, "As I love My Son, so do I love you." Big question here: do we have any way to measure the Father's love for the Son? Yes. "For [the Father] has loved [the Son] before the foundation of the world." So, He has actually loved *you* before the foundation of the world, because He has the same love for you that He has for His Son.

When God the Father looked upon you, He knit you together in your mother's womb with inconceivable tender care. But with excitement, with joy, with longing and anticipation, He said, "I'm so excited to interact with this one. I can't wait until he gets to hear what is in My heart toward him." Get this planted deep within your heart—the eternal Father adores you. The enemy's desire is to steal and kill that affection by lying to you about how the Father feels about you. But God likes you! He is not angry, frustrated, or disappointed. His temperament is not, "Ughhhh! You did it again?" No. The eternal Father says, "Come on, stand back up again because I cannot wait to help you on your journey. I know there are things that hold you back, but someday you've got to start believing one thing—I still want you."

CAUSE AND EFFECT

When it comes to Peter, I picture that, instead of distancing Himself, the eternal One was leaning into Peter during his weakness. The reality of 1 John 4:19 is incredibly profound: passion for the Son of Man is not stirred as you grit your teeth, clench your fists, and scream in pain on the inside, while maintaining a plastic joker smile on the outside. *Ughhhh … okay, I can do this. Ughhhh … I am going to love God with everything that is in me—with my unfeeling heart, my disbelieving soul, my not-understanding mind, and my feeble strength.*

Imagine, if you will, the same type of statement between two people. *Honey, I don't really like you, but we can force it to work. I feel nothing toward you. I don't believe we are right for each other. My thoughts about you are not usually happy thoughts. And I really don't want to put any effort into our relationship— but it should all work out if we force it for a few years.* Like that would ever fly in any other relationship. Yet somehow we consistently believe it can in our relationship with God. But this is not how He set it up.

Let's be honest. We have no ability in ourselves to love God. "We love Him because He first loved us." In other words, I love Jesus because I have experienced His love toward me. I am moved toward Jesus because I have felt Him moving toward me. Passion and longing have been stirred within me because I have felt His passion and longing toward me. We have all heard 1 John 4:19, but do we truly grasp it?

Love is a response. What happens if I come home and my wife is waiting for my car to drive up, just anticipating the minute I get home? All that does is create a greater anticipation in me to get to her. If I see her looking out the window for me, suddenly I'm going 90 mph into my garage. I love my wife because of her love for me; she wins me over. The enemy lies to you about the relentless desire of the Son of Man. That is his goal.

I'm going to make a bold statement here. I think the majority of the Church in the Western world is oblivious to what bursts forth from the heart of the living God. This is the root of the boredom and complacency within the Church walls. We are oblivious to His affection and His longing, yet we are religiously striving to love Him. Love is not in striving; love is a response. Passion for Jesus comes because we have felt His passion. We move toward Jesus because we have felt Him move toward us.

We need to get first things first. We need to understand the setup of God. When we touch the desire that is in His heart, the First Commandment takes its rightful place. When I say First Commandment, I'm talking about the place where your heart is tender and you experience deep longing. I'm talking about the place where your life, money, and time revolve around loving Jesus. It will take more than the ol' college try to make that happen. Radical devotion for the Son of Man only comes when we experience His radical devotion to us.

God has longing and desire for you! And when it breaks through the shame, the deception, and the hard and calloused heart, the rocky places become tender. Your heart becomes tender, and longing is stirred. Words you never imagined saying start to come out of your mouth. "I have no desire to go out and party with my friends tonight; I just want to hear those words again, the ones Jesus spoke to me this morning." This is what it is about. This is why Jesus said, *I will take anything. I will take their sin and the wrath of My Father toward sin upon My body because I want to be able to tell them one thing—I like them.*

A LOVESICK ANTICIPATION

Many are covered with sin and shame. I know I have done some stupid things in my life. I had some sin that I could not get rid of; it hung over me everywhere I went. Then one day its power was broken over my life. I confessed my sin, brought everything to the light, and walked into freedom. But shame still had a hold on me; the enemy was screaming in my ear and condemning me. However, even when sin controlled my life, Jesus was leaning in, saying, "I want you." He knows everything about us. Nothing is a surprise. Nothing is a secret. He is fully aware of our inner lives. And with that knowledge, the Son of Man says, "I want you." In that place, all He wants is our gaze.

In the same way He spoke to the Laodicean church in the book of Revelation, I believe Jesus is speaking to us today. "I wish that you were either hot or cold." He yearns for us to grasp His affection and for that to fuel our affection as we pour it back upon Him. He is calling us back to our place in the vine where we are abiding in Him, a place of intimacy and fellowship. He is calling us to the place of repentance because He wants our gaze, and He will do anything to get it. Do you know why He is even willing to discipline you? Because He loves you, He will do whatever it takes to get your gaze.

Look at it from the Father's perspective. He says, "I want to present a bride to My Son who is completely in love with Him. Oh, Church, you have no idea who this One is, but if you begin to touch the depths of this Man, you will be so awakened for My Son that you will long for His coming."

Human history ends with us, the bride of Christ, calling out for Jesus to come because we are lovesick and cannot wait for the day when He splits the sky. He is coming back, and we, the Church, are going to be there. Nothing is going to be distracting our gaze. He will have a pure and spotless bride. This is the reason of all creation. She will be found wanting, waiting, and ready. She is not going to be concerned about herself, her circumstances, her position, or her posture in life. She has only one concern: the Divine has pierced her, and she is lovesick because she has touched Him. We will be standing there saying, *Jesus, I cannot wait to see You! I cannot wait for the day that my eyes see Yours. Oh, Jesus, You love me, and I love You. I want You to come back. You have wounded me with love, and there is no other place I can turn. I am ruined for anything less. It is about love, Jesus! Come to me!*

At the Passover feast, Peter displayed the intentions of his heart by vowing to die for Jesus. But really, it has always been about living for Him—with an undeniable, overwhelming desire that overshadows everything else. He has all the subservient angels He could want surrounding His throne. What He seeks is a bride who is in love with Him, not because she simply wants to stick to the winning side, but because she has felt His desire for her. She gives love because she has received love from Love Himself. Not only that, but she loves well—it's not lacking in any measure. And she is walking in the fullness of the Godhead, the fullness of love. She may be hard-pressed on every side, but her spirit is vibrant and joyful. She is abiding in the vine, knowing that there is a longing in the Lord's heart for her that never subsides, never relents, never lets go. She is not defined by her sin, but by the Lord as a lover of God who finds herself distracted by the momentary cares of this fallen world.

The Lord will take any willing heart unto Himself. It is simply a matter of prioritizing, allowing passion to take precedence because we know love is eternal. Peter's heart was pierced with the divine, and it made him a lover. It also made him an evangelist, a teacher, and an apostle, but most of all, a man in love with the Son. Even as a betrayer, you were called by Jesus to be His eternal love. You are not defined by your sin; it has not discounted you. You are the delight of God's heart. You are His one thing. His invitation to you is to make Him yours. Be God's. Abide in His love. And love well. This is truly how it is supposed to be.

FROM DESIRE TO ACTION

THE SIMPLICITY OF DESIRE

What really matters in life? That's what this *one thing* stuff is about. It is not about this week, this month, or this year. It is about eternity; it is about reality. When the Bible gives a verse that boils down all of life, it is simpler than you thought it would be. Besides the verses we have looked at in this book, here are a few more.

> *"He has shown you, O man, what is good; and what does the Lord require of you but to do justly, to love mercy, and to walk humbly with your God?" —Micah 6:8, NKJV*

"The conclusion, when all has been heard, is: fear God and keep His commandments, because this applies to every person."
—Ecclesiastes 12:13, NAS

"But you must return to your God; maintain love and justice, and wait for your God always."
—Hosea 12:6, NIV

"But take careful heed to do the commandment and the law which Moses the servant of the Lord commanded you, to love the Lord your God, to walk in all His ways, to keep His commandments, to hold fast to Him, and to serve Him with all your heart and with all your soul." —Joshua 22:5, NKJV

"And he will give you all you need from day to day if you live for him and make the Kingdom of God your primary concern."
—Matthew 6:33, NLT

"And you shall love the Lord your God with all your heart, with all your soul, with all your mind, and with all your strength. This is the first commandment." —Mark 12:30, NKJV

It's amazing how God can cut through all our hardened defenses and expose our hearts. We tend to make it more complicated, creating a labyrinth of spiritual red tape and circus hoops to jump through. All the while, Jesus is asking us if we can just believe what He says. Do we believe He feels deeply for us— deep longing, deep desire, deep love? If we do, it is that much easier to fall in love with Him.

Look at it another way. God sustains every universe in existence. He balances every microscopic detail with consistent precision, knowing infinite information about each element and its interactions. Yet for all the calculations involved, there's no *oops*, no galactic meltdown, no space-time continuum flub. He maintains creation with barely a fraction of His power, but it flourishes as if each component had a personal caretaker. And you are so much more precious!

Let's bring this a little closer to home with a real-world example. I have a friend who was recently fired from his job without warning. The job paid well, was honorable work, and provided for his family. It was a dream job—a cakewalk that he got paid to do. His skills are limited, and, without a cubicle-worthy degree, there are only a small number of options available to him, none of which will help his family get out of debt.

This disruptive transition has brought up a lot of issues, but the details are insignificant compared to the questions concerning his heart. What will he say about this situation? How does he talk about those involved? What does his heart do when he recalls the circumstances? What about depression, bitterness, and negativity? How has this affected his relationship with God? Does God see him any differently now?

The central issue is not my friend's circumstances; it is his heart. It's not about your circumstances either. Your heart is the wellspring from which all else flows (Prov. 4:23)—your outlook on life, your daily attitude, your priorities, goals, and dreams. Your heart governs how you spend your time, energy, and resources as well as what you believe about things like family, right and wrong, justice, and "the great beyond." That's why God is after your heart. You can do a lot through willpower, but when your heart is moved, an otherworldly power is released—it's called love, or desire. Our understanding of romance and longing is a dim picture of how God's heart beats for you, and it is a taste of how He wants your heart to beat toward Him.

He wants your heart to be moved, but not just in any direction. He wants you to be moved toward Him because you are famished. He wants you to take the hunger that resides in your heart and pursue Him with such tenacity that it makes onlookers jealously uncomfortable, stirring the same pursuit inside of them. In Thomas Dubay's book *The Evidential Power of Beauty*, the subjects of hunger, fascination, and pursuit are eloquently considered.

> You and I, each and every one of us without exception, can be defined as an aching need for the infinite. Some people realize this; some do not. But even the latter illustrate this inner ache when, not having God deeply, they incessantly spill themselves out into excitements and experiences, licit or illicit. They are trying to fill their inner emptiness, but they never succeed, which is why the search is incessant. Though worldly pleasure seeking never fulfills and satisfies in a continuing way, it may tend momentarily to distract and to dull the profound pain of the inner void. If these people allow themselves a moment of reflective silence (which they seldom do), they notice a still, small voice whispering, Is this all there is? They begin to sense a thirst to love with abandon, without limit, without end, without lingering aftertastes of bitterness. In other words, their inner spirit is clamoring, even if confusedly, for unending beauty. How they and we respond to this inner outreach rooted in our deep spiritual soul is the

most basic set of decisions we can make: they have eternal consequences.[1]

King David desired one thing. Paul the apostle did one thing. Peter knew one thing. Mary of Bethany chose one thing. The God called Love loved them, and they learned how to love Him back. I am calling you back to the First Commandment, to the greatest invitation ever given. Come, fall in love with the greatest Lover the world has ever known. Give yourself to the simplicity of desire—His desire for you—and watch how yours grows. Regardless of your response, the heavenly Bridegroom, Jesus, pursues you day after day. You are His bride. He delights in you, likes you, and longs for your affection. He is after your heart.

CULTIVATING DESIRE

Have you felt that there could be something more to your Christian walk—something big perhaps? Maybe it's the driving force that causes you to take your next step every morning, day after day. In a word, it is desire. Without it, you just wouldn't take that step. Go without desire for too long, and you will be hard-pressed to come up with a reason to continue on in futility. We have basically discussed the *what* and *why* behind the issues of desire, but now we will take a look at the *how*. How exactly do you go about cultivating a heart of fascination and desire for God? It is good that you have desire, but desire needs to be accompanied by action in order to become a reality. Twenty years of wrong thinking is only changed through the proactive retraining of your mind.

In his book *The Knowledge of the Holy*, A.W. Tozer says something noteworthy:

1. Thomas Dubay, S.M., *The Evidential Power of Beauty* (San Francisco: Ignatius Press, 1999), 17.

What comes into our minds when we think about God is the most important thing about us ... For this reason the gravest question before the Church is always God Himself, and the most portentous fact about any man is not what he at a given time may say or do, but what he in his deep heart conceives God to be like ... Were we able to extract from any man a complete answer to the question, "What comes into your mind when you think about God?" we might predict with certainty the spiritual future of that man. Were we able to know exactly what our most influential religious leaders think of God today, we might be able with some precision to foretell where the Church will stand tomorrow.[2]

David's fascination with and desire for God was the sustaining factor of his life. He ended his spiritual life well, unlike Solomon, who lost his way. David was hunted, persecuted, and defamed; he committed atrocious sins, set up an innocent man to be murdered, had an affair, and caused the Lord's priests to be killed. Yet throughout his seasons of persecution and sin, his hunger for and fascination with God always pulled him through. That is our answer as well.

The prescription I have found for growing in passion and love for Jesus Christ is found in the place of worship using the Scripture. The Bible is alive and active, so interacting with it is the best way to encounter God. Worship, unlike any other act, has the ability to unlock the heart because it flows primarily *from* the heart, and the heart is how you to connect with God. Time and again we are invited to interact with the Holy Spirit concerning God's feelings toward us, using Scripture as the connection point. You are not supposed to read the Bible in

2. A.W. Tozer, *The Knowledge of the Holy* (New York: HarperCollins, 1961), 1.

order to become increasingly moral or to fine-tune the duties of your religious lifestyle, although these will certainly be an overflow of your spiritual life. You are to get before God to feel His passion wash over you and to align yourself with Truth—in short, to have your heart moved.

Satan's desire is to kill, steal, and destroy. He will use any means possible and is more than willing to lie about God and His nature (what He looks like and how He feels toward you). So the purpose of quiet time spent with God is to allow the Truth to continually refine and expand our understanding of Him. In time, the driving force of your daily passion will be finding out what He looks like, who He is, and experiencing Him for yourself.

A BIGGER PICTURE

> *"From one man [God] made every nation*
> *of men, that they should inhabit the whole*
> *earth; and he determined the times set for*
> *them and the exact places where they should*
> *live. God did this so that men would seek him*
> *and perhaps reach out for him and find him,*
> *though he is not far from each one of us."*
> *—Acts 17:26-27, NIV*

The Lord has an enormous plan in the works, and it all springs from His desire to welcome you into eternal love. He determined every miniscule detail about your life, including where and when you would make earth your home. Class status, race, height, gender—He planned it all so that you would search and find Him. It is imperative that this generation understand the bigger picture—experiencing the fullness of God—so that during this

161

age and the age to come, you will find Him, just as the heroes of the faith have. They lived their lives to interact with and experience His endless depths. In the same way, you are invited to feel, experience, trust, and be moved by God. Everything that comes your way—every glory and every pain—is for the purpose of going deeper in your pursuit of Jesus, falling deeper in love with Him.

THE PRESCRIPTION: PRAYING SCRIPTURE

The first step is to get yourself in the place of anointed worship, which I define as whatever stills the clamoring of your soul and causes your heart to move toward God. If you have done this before, don't write it off as "been there, done that." I call you to it again, for there is no greater reward than the human heart experiencing God.

In the place of worship, find a verse that focuses on the nature, attributes, appearance, or feelings of God or on our response to Him. Read it and begin to pray it through. Many people find it helpful to sing the verse as well. Memorize it as much as you can and go over it several times a day. Use some cross-reference tools and really search Him out. You may even choose to carve out times of silence or fasting dedicated solely to Him. We do this all the time at IHOP, and I can tell you with full confidence that the benefits are eternal and glorious.

However you do it, the point is to get the Word inside you so it contributes to the core of who you are and positions you to feel Him. I'll say that again: the Word within you positions you to feel Him, the source of desire. When we feel His desire for us, we start to feel desire for Him. Imagine if all week a wife opened the door to a clean house sprinkled with flowers, a table full of handwritten love notes, and surprise for-no-reason-at-all gifts. When a time set aside from kids and cares arrives, the words *loved much* have no doubt been resonating within her heart. Because the truth of her husband's love has been spoken to her in many ways, her desire is awakened for him. So intense is Jesus' love for you, He left untainted Glory just to win one glance of your eyes so you could see heaven in His, so you could receive the truth, so you could enter into Desire.

It really is pretty simple: worship, read, pray, sing, and allow a few minutes of breathing room for Him to touch you. You are being changed by the Truth. Here is an example of how I might pray from Psalm 27:4: *As David had a desire for only You, I'm asking that this desire be stirred in me. Just as he stood in awe and fascination of You, I long to be fascinated. This is a true cry, Father: I want to touch You and experience You. I put myself before You, for I want to know and understand You. Just as David spoke of beholding Your beauty, reveal Your beauty to me, that I would behold it. That which keeps the angels fascinated—fascinate me with it. Whether I feel You today or not, I know that You are the God who hears prayer. Amen.*

He's waiting to speak to the hunger of your heart, to change your duty to delight, to turn your "ought to" into your "want to." Here is a list of verses to get you started.

- o **Psalm 16:11**
- o **Psalm 17:7**
- o **Psalm 18**
- o **Psalm 27:4**
- o **Psalm 36:7-10**
- o **Psalm 43:3**
- o **Psalm 66:3-7**
- o **Psalm 73:25-26**

o Psalm 118:1
o Psalm 139:1-18
o Song of Solomon 5:10-16
o Isaiah 9:6-7
o Isaiah 11:10
o Isaiah 53:1-12
o Isaiah 62:2-5
o Micah 6:8
o Zephaniah 3:17
o John 17:24-26
o 1 Corinthians 2:6-12
o Ephesians 1:16-19
o Ephesians 3:16-20
o Colossians 1:15-22
o Hebrews 2:9-11, 14-18
o Hebrews 5:7-9
o 1 John 4:7-8, 18-19
o Revelation 1:13-16
o Revelation 4:2-5
o Revelation 5:5-13
o Revelation 15:3-4

THE VALUE OF PERSEVERANCE

Don't get caught up in making vows about the next ten years of your life. Start with today or just this week, with the understanding that you intend to go the long haul. When you mess up, forget, or get busy, simply adjust your focus back to Jesus and start again. At IHOP we say, "Push delete and start over." It really is that simple. The day may come when you feel the Spirit prompting you to make a greater vow, but it will be accompanied by a special grace for that purpose. Until then, pursue Him today with your best.

If you find that "nothing is happening," instruction, education, and inspiration can certainly help in redefining and countering wrong concepts of God. However, God gave us His Word. So while other tools may have cool or interesting *ways* to say things, He actually has interesting *things* to say. The majestic and loving King of creation is waiting to touch you and commune with you in a way unmatched by another human's abilities. It is God we are after; it is God we need; and we must get Him for ourselves. After all, He is our great reward. Teaching and instruction can be an aid, but God often allows you to experience dry times to cause you to "grope that you may find Him."

Perseverance in the journey is of great value, and it is handsomely rewarded from the abundance of heaven. At the end of the day, we are called to persevere through a little difficulty now because the truth, and our exceedingly great reward, is that "God is not far from each one of us."

Many early mornings, I pray for this young adult generation, specifically for you. I want to close this book by offering up a prayer from Ephesians 1:15-19 for you as you begin making this day different. May you make Jesus your one thing more and more, and may you truly understand the eternal depths of His love for you.

Father of glory, reveal Your glory. May the eyes of their understanding be opened today, that they would arise to the hope of Your calling over their lives. Let them understand the riches of Your glory, Your inheritance in us, and the exceeding greatness of Your power toward us. Heavenly Father, I am asking for the spirit of revival to be loosed, that the message of the excellencies of Christ would be proclaimed, that we would truly see lives moved toward You in wholeheartedness. I am praying that desire and longing—true passion—would be stirred. Turn hearts toward Your glorious Son.

I'm asking now that You would prepare a bride. Awaken and stir her; restore identity back to her. Move hearts toward Your Son this hour. On university campuses, in workplaces, and in high schools, brood over believers and non-believers alike. Release the spirit of revelation, that we would see hearts turned toward Your Son.

Father, make Your Son glorious this hour; make Him known. We want the knowledge of God to spread. I'm asking that You give young adults supernatural encounters. Apprehend them and awaken them this hour with dreams and visions. I'm asking that You would move mightily. I lay hold of You for a great awakening of hearts. I want hearts stirred with longing, hearts stirred with desire. We want the Spirit of God; we want hearts revived and renewed in the Man, Jesus. Do not delay!

Father, we're in need! I'm asking now that You turn the disillusionment, the disconnectedness, and the bewilderment into fascination. Turn it into wonder and awe. We're asking You to come, to save, to move for the glory of Your name. Smash deception and demonic strongholds. Make known Your resurrecting power. Let the Son of Man arise in beauty. Proclaim the excellencies of Christ throughout this nation.

Holy Spirit, I'm asking now for Your aid in advancing the glory of Jesus. Eternal Father, say the word—let revelation run rampant through this land. Let there be a great awakening of hearts with fascination. Jesus, make Your excellencies known. Awaken hearts for Yourself. Amen.

IHOP
MISSIONS BASE

INTERNATIONAL HOUSE OF PRAYER
Kansas City

- 24/7 prayer and worship since September of 1999.

- Forerunner School of Ministry: Full-time Bible school with dynamic theological teaching founded upon intimacy with Jesus.

- Internships: Short-term training programs of three to six months include Young Adult Internships, International Internships, the Simeon Company, Fire in the Night and Summer Teen Internships.

- IHOP-KC is composed of 400 staff members, 700 Forerunner School of Ministry students and hundreds of interns, operating within a unique nonstop "furnace" committed to prayer, fasting and persistent pursuit of the Lord.

www.ihop.org

ONETHING

Onething is more than a conference. It is a ministry set upon seeing a great awakening in regard to hearts coming alive to the true nature of God.

Onething is a young-adult ministry stemming from the International House of Prayer-Kansas City. We at Onething have a specific message and carry a mandate to call young adults to return to their primary purpose in this life. We are endeavoring to see the First Commandment lived out in wholehearted passion for Jesus.

Our desire is to pierce hearts with the truth of this Man, Jesus, causing chains to fall off, eyes to be opened and complacent hearts to be revived as wholehearted lovers of Jesus.

"One thing I have desired, and that will I seek." —Psalm 27:4

What do you desire?

www.ihop.org

[RELEVANTBOOKS]

FOR MORE INFORMATION ABOUT OTHER RELEVANT BOOKS,
check out www.relevantbooks.com.